COCKTAIL
CULTURE

COCKTAIL CULTURE

MARK KINGWELL

DESIGNED & DECORATED BY SETH

PORTOBELLO 2007

Published by Portobello Books Ltd 2007

Portobello Books Ltd
Eardley House
4 Uxbridge Street
Notting Hill Gate
London W8 7SY, UK

First published in Canada by McClelland & Stewart in 2006

A CIP catalogue record is available from the British Library

9 8 7 6 5 4 3 2 1

ISBN 978 1 84627 114 4

www.portobellobooks.com

Typeset in Bembo by M&S, Toronto

Printed in The Netherlands by Krips bv.

For Eddie, Joe, Gary, and Nick

"Let me prepare it for you, if I may . . .
Strong . . . but sip it slowly . . . and drink it sitting down."
— T.S. Eliot, *The Cocktail Party*

CONTENTS

ACKNOWLEDGEMENTS

My thanks go first and foremost to Derek Finkle, editor of *Toro* magazine, who called me up a few years ago with the unexpected idea of writing a drinks column for his then-fledgling men's magazine. I was already in debt to Derek for his successfully persuading me to grow back my hair after some years spent shaving my head. This had the effect of making me appear marginally younger and, maybe more valuable, no longer terrifying to my little niece Aidan. Now I have yet another reason to thank Derek: the magazine has been a huge success, and the column went with it, among other things to a National Magazine Award.

Thanks, too, to Melanie Morassutti and the other staffers at the magazine for saving me, over and over, from the usual quota of factual errors, grammatical infelicities, and untenable opinions.

The incomparable Seth illustrated the first six columns I wrote, after which the job was taken over by Studio Lucha and their beautiful retro silkscreens. When it came to this book, I knew Seth's work would offer the perfect complement for the text, as well as making the resulting volume everything a writer could hope for, namely, a work of art in its own right.

My father, my brothers Sean and Steve, Julian Siggers, Fred Hawkshaw, Bruce Montgomery, Molly Montgomery, Lavinia Greenlaw, Chloe Puton, and Georgia Ardizzone acted as test subjects for some of these mixes. I thank them all. Joel Dubin, Barry McCartan, Cynthia Macdonald, Sean Foran, and Matthew Parfitt were there early and deserve some kind of credit.

Thanks to Chris Bucci and Doug Pepper of McClelland & Stewart, who wanted to publish this book as much as I did. Doug, a cocktail aficionado of note in at least two countries, favours something called the Corpse Reviver No. 2. He will make you one if you ask him nicely, sometimes even during a meeting.

A fine drink, certainly; but in tribute to the house, this year celebrating a hundred years of publishing quality Canadian literature, here is an almost-forgotten drink as acknowledgement: The McClelland Cocktail (from *The New York Bartender's Guide*; sorry, there is no Stewart). Combine four parts sloe gin with two parts white curaçao and a dash of absinthe, or three to five dashes of orange bitters if absinthe is not ready to your hand. Shake with cracked ice and strain into a chilled cocktail glass. Garnish with a cherry and a twist of lemon. Here's to a hundred more years.

Thanks, finally, to pretty much everyone I know for teaching me, either by example or by implication, the ancient virtue of moderation – itself properly observed in moderation. Saint Augustine said: *Multi quidem facilius se abstinent ut non utantur, quam temperent ut bene utantur.* Not for us the path of that multitude.

INTRODUCTION

The Theory and Practice of Drink, in Five Parts

"My dear, this is a fashionable London parish, so called,"
said Randolph. He carved the saddle of mutton savagely, as
if he were rending his parishioners. "What hope is there
for them this Lent? I suppose they can give up drinking
cocktails."
– Barbara Pym, *An Unsuitable Attachment* (1982)

A few years ago Conan O'Brien, the former television host
and comedy producer, was asked to give a Class Day speech at
Harvard University, his alma mater. He was a hit. Among other

things, he described the lifelong burden of having attended the famous Ivy League finishing school in Cambridge, Mass. "You see," O'Brien told the long rows of smiling grads, "you're in for a lifetime of 'and you went to Harvard?' Accidentally give the wrong amount of change in a transaction and it's, 'and you went to Harvard?' Ask the guy at the hardware store how these jumper cables work and hear, 'and you went to Harvard?' Forget just once that your underwear goes inside your pants and it's 'and you went to Harvard?' Get your head stuck in your niece's dollhouse because you wanted to see what it was like to be a giant and it's 'Uncle Conan, and you went to Harvard!?'"

Now, I didn't go to Harvard myself. I went to Yale, where nobody expects anything of you except the occasional presidency. Still, I think I understand what O'Brien was telling the happy one-percenters as they got set to venture out into the world beyond the high-percentile security fence. I may not have gone to Harvard, but I am a philosopher.

For reasons that remain unclear, people outside the academic walls balk at the label "philosopher" in a manner not applied to "historian," "political scientist," or "physicist." At the same time, curiously, everyone from defensive coordinators and garage mechanics to graphic designers and cooks speaks regularly about their "philosophy" of this or that: the nickel defence, fuel injection systems, white space, fusion spicing. As a result of this curious combination of normative escalation and commonplace lowering, mere philosophers – by which I just mean those of us whose lucky profession it is to teach the great traditions of human inquiry – are caught in a weird judgmental vertigo. We are not supposed to admit interests that fail some notional standard of intellectual seriousness; instead we are supposed to behave as if (in the great Vulcan inversion) we were dead from the neck down. Nobody knows who commands this standard, or why, but its dicta are clear.

Admit you watch kung fu movies or *The Simpsons* and it's, "and you're a philosopher?" Let slip your interest in college football or NASCAR and it's, "and you're a philosopher?" Confess a casual liking for suede sneakers or Cary Grant's suits and it's, "and you're a philosopher?" Cocktails? A fatal lack of seriousness. This sort of judgment is distinct from those standard expressions of wonderment that a philosopher cannot change a tire, put up drywall, or find coordinates on a map. Whereas unworldliness confirms philosophical status, but only negatively, as a joke, worldliness disconfirms it as "serious." Gotcha, and double gotcha!

Some people, obviously, have an interest in the subject of cocktails. For most of us, it is hardly an overpowering or obsessional calling. This interest is not merely theoretical, in that we like drinking drinks as well as writing about them. It is likewise not theoretical in another sense, because, despite the title of this introduction, we do not have, nor do we believe there to be, some Big Theory of cocktails. There is no philosophy of mixology.

One could of course subject cocktails to moral or sociological analysis, or both. One could, for example, place them in the same frame of "taste" and "production of consumption" as analyzed by Thorstein Veblen in his classic study *The Theory of the Leisure Class* (1899). The gentleman of leisure, Veblen says, "becomes a connoisseur in creditable viands of various degrees of merit, in manly beverages and trinkets, in seemly apparel and architecture, in weapons, games, dances, and narcotics. This cultivation of the aesthetic faculty requires time and application, and the demands made upon the gentleman in this direction therefore tend to change his life of leisure into a more or less arduous application to the business of learning how to live a life of ostensible leisure in a becoming way."

This book does not take "manly beverages" seriously in that sense, and does not have much time for people who do. Such seriousness is, among other things, boring. The relevant other things include self-defeating, and tautological: first leisure becomes work, and then all judgments are reduced to claims of status. Note also the meta-irony first remarked by the late John Kenneth Galbraith, that only the scholarly, which is to say those who enjoy either private or state-sponsored leisure, have time to read Veblen! We will not bother to argue here the obvious truth that all scales of value have their own fatal self-contradictory blind spots, usually just about exactly where their holder is standing. Baseball games, no; art openings, yes. A cufflink collection, bad; a power tool collection, good. Video games, nasty; foreign films, uplifting. Every puritan is a dandy of his own convictions – and, of course, vice versa.

For what it's worth, philosophers have long had an abiding interest in drink, if not always as served shaken and strained into a chilled glass. For anthropological and historical reasons, they tend to prefer wine. Everyone knows that Plato's most appealing dialogue, *Symposium*, is a record of a drinking party where the vinous talk turned to love. Alcibiades, who comes late and drunk to the party, notes that one of Socrates' many virtues is that he can drink anybody under the table. This famous capacity is just one reason Socrates has got under the Athenian golden boy's skin.

Drink and other mood-altering substances have figured in many other corners of the tradition. Thomas Aquinas enjoyed his wine and his food with such unbridled gusto that a special table had to be fashioned for him, with an arc carved out to accommodate his ample paunch. Immanuel Kant, despite his reputation for deadly seriousness and strict insistence on moral duty, was a dedicated dandy and dinner-party *bon vivant* for most of his life. David Hume, who warned against the dangers of self-medication when in the throes of skeptical vertigo, nevertheless enjoyed a healthy and bibulous social life. His broad red Scottish face got redder still, we are told, when he was deep in his cups.

"My company was not unacceptable to the young and careless, as well as to the studious and literate," Hume avers in an autobiographical sketch composed just before his death; "and as I took a particular pleasure in the company of modest women, I had no reason to be displeased with the reception I met with from them." Hume was in this, as in all things, eminently sane. The same cannot be said for his mad contemporary Bishop George Berkeley, whose notorious experiments with "medicinal" tar-water and other crude hallucinogens were an attempt, centuries before Aldous Huxley or Timothy Leary, to open wider the doors of perception.

Berkeley's example suggests that one sort of "philosophical" defence of cocktails might consist in an argument about the twinned goals of sociable loquacity and consciousness-expansion. Liquor loosens the tongue and opens the mind! Insofar as all philosophy may be considered an attempt at changing the shape of consciousness (even unto consciousness *about* consciousness), philosophy and booze are natural partners. One might even be considered incomplete without the other. *Nunc est bibendum!* as they say in Latin. (Loosely rendered: *Let's get toasted!*)

In reality, such a claim makes a dangerous linkage, and probably describes a slippery slope to boot. After all, why stop at booze or even mild hallucinogens if the goal is some notional "mind-expansion"? Why not continue down the road to major self-fucking-up on the order of *Altered States* (1980), where William Hurt's psychologist character uses peyote and a sensory-deprivation tank to regress into a violent lower-order primate? Even a philosopher can recognize that as crazy. We offer, instead, a different kind of suggestion for altering consciousness, one that has the linked benefits of being more specific to cocktails (rather than wine, about which much has already been written) and less obviously self-serving to the already committed stoner (who should not really be encouraged).

This book is not for you if you think drinking in the afternoon is wrong, or if the thought of dealing with a hangover by mixing a stinger is repugnant. We take it that most new-millennium people do not drink the way their parents (or grandparents) might have done, at least as presented in, say, Sloan Wilson's classic of post-war salaryman angst, *The Man in the Gray Flannel Suit* (1955). In this influential novel about the Manhattan bedroom communities of Connecticut, later a Gregory Peck film, people start drinking at lunchtime, have an after-work martini at the bar in Grand Central Terminal, one on the train, and yet another as soon as they get home. Then they go to a party. "On Greentree Avenue cocktail parties started at seven-thirty, when the men came home from New York, and they usually continued without any dinner until three or four o'clock in the morning," the narrator says. "Somewhere around nine-thirty in the evening, Martinis and Manhattans would give way to highballs, but the formality of eating anything but hors d'oeuvres in-between had been entirely omitted."

Let it be said: that is not a good idea. The basic premise of the present book is that you should choose your drink carefully, take some care in its preparation, and enjoy it in moderation. Drinking cocktails is supposed to be fun, but not *too much* fun. Cocktails are associated with sophistication, after all, and whatever you may think in your own mind, you are not sophisticated after more than two stiff drinks.

Moderation will not always be your watchword in practice; we accept that. If inebriation should occur, at least try to stay cheerful – nobody likes a mean drunk or a belligerent one. Drink takes people different ways at different times, as Damon Runyon's "Stages of Drunkenness" usefully illustrates. The stages, as told to Dan Jenkins of *Sports Illustrated* magazine, are these:

1. witty and charming
2. rich and powerful
3. philosophical
4. against the designated hitter
5. f— dinner
6. witty and charming, part II
7. for the designated hitter

8. morose and despondent

9. invisible

10. bulletproof

There is probably some optimal cocktail equilibrium to be found somewhere between (3) and (4), though we agree it can be difficult to halt momentum in this regard. Stage (5) is clearly the point at which things may begin to go decisively wrong, despite the manifest virtues of (6) and the solid wisdom of (7) if you happen to live in an American League city.

We offer this list purely in the spirit of caution. We all know there are consequences even for the invisible, though that knowledge often lacks deterrent effect. "Fred," the narrator of Truman Capote's novella *Breakfast at Tiffany's* (1958) – whose Audrey Hepburn/George Peppard 1961 film version features one of the best cocktail-party scenes on celluloid – offers this assessment of the risk. Mag Wildwood, Holly Golightly's six-foot-tall model friend, has one drink too many. "Suddenly she was blind," "Fred" says. "And since gin to artifice bears the same relation as tears to mascara, her attractions at once dissembled." That is a precise corollary of *in vino veritas* that some of us would prefer to avoid seeing demonstrated.

"Fred" (that is, Paul Jarvik in the film, nameless but clearly Capote in the book) is no teetotaller. When he gets a publishing advance, he celebrates with Holly by starting with two rounds of manhattans in one bar and then moving on to champagne cocktails in another – not recommended. He pays the price with a dose of what Holly calls "the mean reds" the next morning. That condition is not synonymous with hangover, but often enough accompanies it, alcohol being after all a somatic depressive as well as a disinhibitor. P.G. Wodehouse recognized this, even if he took a rather lighter view of things. There is so much drinking in Wodehouse that we might be forgiven for thinking that the only people who put away more than post-war Americans were pre-war Englishmen – which hypothesis we have not, despite much effort, found it possible to test.

Though the drinks mostly are plain, on the order of whisky or brandy with soda taken pretty much any hour of the day, the Wodehouse universe is rich in spiffing and colourful phrases for drunkenness, too, a Joycean range extending well beyond the usual options of hammered, toasted, loaded, and bagged that most of us consider sufficient. Consider: awash; fried to the tonsils; full to the back teeth; lathered; lit a bit; mopping the stuff up to some extent; off-colour; oiled; ossified; pie-eyed; plastered; polluted; primed to the sticking point; scrooched; shifting it a bit; sozzled; squiffy; stewed; stinko; suffering from magnums; tanked to the uvula; tight as an owl; under the sauce; under the surface; whiffled; woozled; and, finally, stirring the green swizzle.

Wodehouse knew that a stiff drink is not just a pleasure; sometimes it is a necessity. For example, before a public speech. "If you want real oratory, the preliminary noggin is essential," Bertie Wooster asserts. "Unless pie-eyed, you cannot hope to grip." Sometimes you simply require generalized picking-up. "The barman recommended a lightning whizzer, an invention of his own. He said it was what rabbits trained on when they were matched against grizzly bears and there was only one instance on record of the bear having lasted three rounds." And then there are moments when your liver just seems to crave a bit of a caning. "He tottered blindly towards the bar," Bertie remarks of one honourable member of the Drones Club, "like a camel making for an oasis after a hard day at the office."

It should be no surprise that Wodehouse likewise understood the nature of morning-after consequences. More than just lamenting them, he offered a catalogue of six distinct hangover modalities. There is, he suggested, the Broken Compass, the Sewing Machine, the Comet, the Atomic, the Cement Mixer, and, of course, the Gremlin Boogie.

Which naturally raises the issue of the hangover cure. There is, as everybody knows, no cure for the hangover except time itself. But some additional steps may be taken, either in calm prospect or in desperate recourse. Lots of water during and after drinking, plus maybe two Advil before bed, will take care of most nascent Cement Mixers. If that fails, you have the option of post-mortem food or post-mortem drink. The key here, obviously, is to find a specific that stops short of emetic. If you opt for food, you face a further choice between (a) a fat-and-carb blast in the shape of stacked pancakes and a bacon-cheeseburger; or (b) attempted health-maintenance via Gatorade, orange juice, and a banana. The Wodehouse version of the former is, apparently, a dozen lamb chops and a battered pudding from the Drones Club dining room. The latter's potassium and other essentials will help you there, but there's no substitute for calories when the body is beaten down. Adding exercise to the regime – a popular if misguided option – entails the uncomfortable paradox that sweating away nasty impurities is accomplished only at the cost of further dangerous dehydration.

Drink is simpler, and more reliable. For there is no remedy more effective than a brief re-entry into that medieval medical wisdom that suggests a philtre fashioned from the hair of the dog that bit you. It is probably best to avoid the crisis-moment measures of a character in a Kingsley Amis novel, an American, who deals with his morning ills by simply lifting the vodka bottle to his lips and gargling.

Jeeves, Bertie Wooster's incomparable valet, or "gentleman's private gentleman," is a man of parts, as all readers of Wodehouse have reason to know. In addition to prodigious feats of cogitation, stern fashion sense, and a comprehensive grasp of wagering, Jeeves commands two powerful cures for what Bertie is apt to call "the morning head." One of these is referred to, misleadingly, as a Corpse Reviver – for there is a distinct cocktail, indeed two of them by that name (see our entry on the zombie for details). Jeeves's "Corpse Reviver" is really a species of Bloody Mary, with extra hot sauce, Worcestershire sauce, and egg yolks. Jeeves confesses to Bertie's Aunt Dahlia with becoming modesty that he has never actually tried it on a corpse, but supposes it effective on anybody short of an Egyptian mummy. After the initial raw effect of causing the drinker's eyeballs to pop from their parent sockets and ricochet off the opposite wall, it settles down to its good work. Drinking one, Bertie says, "felt as if someone had touched off a bomb inside the old bean and was strolling down my throat with a lighted torch."

The second Jeeves cure is referred to simply as "the Special" or "the Classic." (The latter not to be confused with a gin-and-tonic of the same name perfected by a certain Washington lawyer we know, who likes to serve them after a hard day spent lounging by the lake in New Hampshire.) No details of the Jeeves Special are given in the Wodehouse writings, though we do know that Bertie credits this "rare and refreshing" tipple with the power to turn a lamb into a lion – and, indeed, vice versa.

Speaking of gin and tonic, you might wish to heed instead the wisdom of Charlie Mortdecai, the disreputable art dealer, sometime spy and cultured hero of Kyril Bonfiglioli's under-appreciated crime novels of the 1970s (see the entry on "Spygames"). Mortdecai's bodyguard and manservant, Jock, "allowed me one of his Salvation Specials, which have been known to twitch a man back from the very brink of the grave." What is this marvellous potable contrivance? "No Jeevesean Worcester sauce and raw eggs for Jock: his potion is simply a Dexedrine dissolved in gin and tonic to which he adds a spoonful of Mr. Andrew's noted Liver Salts, two effervescing Vitamin C tablets and two ditto Alka-Seltzer. I have little time for foreigners but I must say that Drs. Alka and Seltzer should have won the Nobel Prize years ago; my only quarrel with their brain-child is its *noise* . . ."

Of course, in a pinch, drink anything. "I have heard it said that a little Pastis is sovereign in these cases. Drives away the evil humours," a defrocked priest tells afflicted Mortdecai early one particularly nasty morning-after. "My better judgment rebelled," Mortdecai notes, "but, as ever, my better judgment received what Jock calls a 'root up the sump' and soon the Pastis was smoothing out the wrinkles in my spleen in cavalry style. When the door-bell rang, two drinks later, I hardly jumped at all."

Like many people, I became fascinated by cocktails long before I was legally able to drink them. I saw them in movies, read about them in books, even now and then observed my parents' friends drinking them from a vantage at the top of the stairs I shared with my older brother. The air force circuit parties of the 1970s probably did not rival the scenes we imagined unfolding in Manhattan studios or on Locust Bay terraces, but the plaid trousers, chiffon dresses, faux-Serpico moustaches, and upswept hair were as close as we could come to glamour while sitting there in our paisley-pattern pyjamas and striped terry-cloth bathrobes.

The gimlet was the first mixed drink I ever tasted, and I blame Raymond Chandler and my brother Steve. Steve loaned me his copy of Chandler's novel *The Long Goodbye* (1953) somewhere around 1978, when I was in high school. He may have received the book in turn from our friend Ed Schmidtke, in which case I blame him too. The sound of Philip Marlowe's hard-bitten, funny *noir* narration, much-imitated but inimitable, remains a benchmark of masculine instability. Though I had never tasted a sip of anything stronger than root beer, I felt I knew exactly what Marlowe meant when he referred to a client as having a "three-highball voice." Marlowe, with his rock-ribbed sense of honour and cement chin, is such a familiar tough-guy figure – depicted cinematically by, among others, Humphrey Bogart, Robert Mitchum, and Elliott Gould – that we sometimes forget the wounded sensibility and moral disgust that lie beneath the tough surface of his *weltschmerzlich* literary voice. When Philip Marlowe recommends a drink, you pay attention, because you know he is the kind of lonely warrior who drinks mostly in pain. For a number of post-adolescent years, I confused the gimlet and the gibson because Marlowe, consistently order-ing the former in *The Long Goodbye*, suddenly favours the latter in *Playback* (1958), Chandler's last novel. (See the entries on these two to note that they are not at all alike, except in being composed almost entirely of gin.)

In the case of my brother and myself, military brats trotted from base to base every three years and obsessed with Camels, Spitfires, Sabres, and Voodoos, Marlowe's status was boosted even further by the fact that Chandler, creator and master of that jaded L.A. voice, was one of those Americans who, like William Faulkner, had joined the Canadian Expeditionary Force during the First World War. Soon after arriving in Europe, Chandler transferred to the Royal Flying Corps. The latter jauntily named operation was the origin of what would later become the Royal Air Force and, in the traditional colonial split, the Royal Canadian Air Force, our father's then-employer. It is one of the minor ironies of literary history that Chandler, though American, attended Dulwich College in England, the very same institution that hosted P.G. Wodehouse as a student before he left to work, briefly, at a bank – experiences rendered into fiction in his early "Mike" and "Psmith" stories, respectively. Chandler (b. 1888) probably never met Wodehouse (b. 1881) at Dulwich, which means neither was able to deploy Bingo Little's favourite piece of moral leverage when trying to enlist Bertie Wooster in a hare-brained romantic scheme: "Bertie, we were at school together." (Bertie: "It wasn't my fault.")

Anyway, the gimlet is an excellent drink, but in common with many fine cocktails it is very strong, and hence not for the weak. Cocktails fascinate in part because they are dangerous. The siren call of glamour can all too easily turn shrill and sloppy, even wicked. In Rona Jaffe's novel *The Best of Everything* (1958), for example, the young career girls of Manhattan navigate the layered byways of wolfish bosses, ambitious rivals, and nearly constant martini drinking. Long before the cosmopolitan fashion of *Sex and the City* and its long comet-tail of associated chick-lit imitators, which made late-century New York into a kind of fantasyland of tits and tippling, Jaffe's funny, sad, clear-eyed tale of affairs, abortions, and advancement nailed the peculiar up-and-down thrills of the urban scene.

Consider beautiful April Morrison, just twenty-two and fresh from the West, who stumbles into a high-society romance with Dexter Key, a good-looking cad blessed with a white jaguar convertible, a country-club lineage, and a Manhattan apartment. Driving into the city from the club, April dissolves into an intoxicated happiness. "This was New York," she thinks to herself, "beside her, Dexter Key; and the marvelous secret things people did inside those tall buildings at the cocktail hour were the things he did every evening, and tonight it was going to happen to her." Not to last, alas (see entry on the gibson). Later, when April is on the skids, she thinks of alcohol a different way, to numb the thought that she has become easy. "She was so humiliated that she wanted to get right up out of bed, but it was too late" – too late because there is already somebody in there with her, someone she barely knows. "So she kept her eyes closed tightly and summoned up the feeling the gin had given her, the feeling that it didn't really matter because life was so much fun, so much fun." It may or may not signify that, when April finally meets a boy who loves her truly, she switches to vodka martinis.

Gin or vodka, the martini has become a cocktail-synecdoche for bourgeois pleasure, a staple of suburban-angst exposés such as Richard Yates's *Revolutionary Road* (1961) or Grace Metalious's *Peyton Place* (1956), later a 1957 Lana Turner film, as well as a television series that paved the way for the modern soap opera. Indeed, in our own day there is a mostly harmless confusion of the martini with cocktails generally, as if the specific drink were a generic descriptor such as Kleenex or Coke. Maybe as a result of these two associations combining, the martini is now even accepted as a symbol of late-capitalist consumption generally, if not American imperialism itself. When I was living in New York in 2002, a popular sign to be seen during protests against the World Trade Organization that spring read, "Bad Capitalist! No Martini!" A sly *New Yorker* cartoon from the same period, echoing a popular post-9/11 justification, made the point from the other side. Well-dressed man to his barroom companion: "The way I look at it, if I don't have that second martini, the terrorists win."

There was indeed an awful lot of drinking going on in New York in those days, maybe more than anytime since the cocktail-party heyday of the 1950s. A good deal of cocaine-snorting and empty sex, too, or so we understand, though nobody has yet written gleeful novels about it the way they did of 1980s Manhattan. All this consumption had a driven air, which was compounded by the realization that, in the clash of civilizations, one side was addicted to alcohol as well as oil: possibly the largest unspoken lifestyle difference between the West and the Rest. (Some parts of the Rest may well be addicted to an even more powerful drug, religious zealotry; but this is not the place to discuss any of that.) Part of any interest in drink is noticing how deeply it has folded itself into the routine narratives of the American Dream, especially as they go toxic in big cities.

New York, as a central feature of American mythopoeisis, figures everywhere in the culture of drink, just as it does in cultural production more generally. But New York falls down on one crucial issue, which is the invention of the cocktail. Indeed, though there are numerous claims that, like jazz and baseball, this is an American innovation, there is far more evidence that the cocktail is an Old World legacy. Various flips, nogs, shrubs, punches, and sangarees had of course been around for many centuries, some of them on record since the Middle Ages. Various forms of mixed drink were popular with the naval officers of Jane Austen's day or the undergraduates of Cardinal Newman's. The modern cocktail descends from these convivial concoctions via the same reasoning that created them, namely that lots of available drink is poor in quality and, especially with rough English gin, in need of palatable covering. Also that, traditionally, it was good etiquette to mix a batch of drinks and then serve them out to your assembled guests: hence the cocktail shaker. An American periodical of 1806 seems to be the first usage of *cocktail* in the modern sense of a mixed drink using hard liquor and flavouring. "A cocktail," they say, "is a stimulating liquor composed of spirits of any kind, sugar, water and bitters." Happy bicentennial, cocktail!

So much is uncontroversial. Whence the name *cocktail*, though? There are as many theories as drinks, and we have no intention of trying to settle the matter here. As lawyers will sometimes bolster a case by adducing multiple, sometimes contradictory arguments, so our view is that in this case *more is more*. A few contenders, from the plausible to the absurd:

1. A mix of champagne and brandy, the original champagne cocktail, was popular in the Bordeaux region as early as the eighteenth century. It was known as a *coquetel*.

2. The practice of "docking" horses, i.e., cutting their tails for show work, often indicates that the animal in question is of mixed breed, not a thoroughbred. The resulting "cocked tail" signals mixture, hence by association mixed drink.

3. A variant version of (2), namely the suggestion that the

centuries-old expression "with cocked tail" describes a horse – or person – displaying high spirits. It naturally follows that a beverage seen to raise people's spirits would be called a cocktail. Naturally.

4. In the southern United States, where cock-fighting was regularly practised, a fighting bird was given a pre-bout lift to its tail with the administration of a slug of hard liquor. (Corollary theory: the winning bird was given the tipple postbout, as a reward for winning. Arguably a wiser strategy.)

5. During the American War of Independence, the owner of a guest house, Betsy Flanagan, regularly housed the officers of Lafayette's and Washington's armies. On one occasion she fed the hungry soldiers by stealing a chicken (*var.* a capon) from her pro-English neighbours and roasting it. To celebrate the theft, she decorated the glasses used during dinner – which contained a sweetened mixture of available drink – with the slaughtered bird's feathers. Her French guests toasted the innovation with a happy cry of: "Vive le cock-tail!"

6. If that sounds ridiculous – which it should – how about the tale of an eccentric doctor named Peynaud, resident of 1880s New Orleans, who used to serve a potent elixir to the customers of his apothecary. He preferred to serve the portions in small egg cups, known as "*coquetiers*." This elegant French word was then mangled by his American friends, and the name for the cup transferred per metonymy to its contents, a cocktail.

7. Our personal favourite. The beautiful daughter of King Axolotl VIII of Mexico was called Xoctl. She was hospitable as well as fetching, and used to prepare the most exquisite drinks for the American visitors to her father's court. Because their crude tongues could not wrap themselves around her lovely name, they called her – and hence, once more via metonymy, her creations – "Cocktail."

It's easier to spell too.

So who is this book for? Well, it is for people who like drinks. That is, those happy creatures who agree with Dr. Johnson that "there is nothing which has yet been contrived by man, by which so much happiness is produced as by a good tavern"; who think, sometimes anyway, that a barstool may be considered "the throne of human felicity."

More particularly, this book is for anyone who thinks cocktails are interesting, including in that interest how they work their way into the cultural imagination, and why, in the end, some of us drink them. Our subject is more the cultural deployment of cocktails than cocktails as such, if that makes any sense. In an old episode of the animated television series *The Simpsons* – the show that launched Conan O'Brien's career, even though he went to Harvard – Bart's teacher, Mrs. Krabappel, momentarily reveals the contents of her drawer of seized classroom contraband. Shoved among the slingshots and firecrackers is a copy of *Playdude* magazine, with the subject line of its "serious" article visible on the cover: "Updike on the Martini." Unlike some, that joke makes you wish the article actually existed.

This book is not a comprehensive guide to cocktails, of which there are many examples already available. We will not give you basic instructions about what equipment to buy, what ingredients to stock, and so on. That stuff strikes us as obvious – though there are always incidental joys to be had in perusing old examples of this step-by-step genre. We fancy particularly long-forgotten volumes such as *Corned Beef and Caviar*, by Marjorie Hillis and Bertina Foltz (1937), a manual that set out level-headed advice for the single city girl trying to make do on a budget and attract a husband. "More than one young man is trying to make it his business to see that she doesn't live alone after his next raise in salary," the authors say of their target reader.

After the fashion of the day, wilted lettuce and consommé play a large part in the menus. In Chapter Six, on "Wine, Women and Cheese," the authors offer this dictum: "You will need a cocktail shaker, preferably one with a removable top so that you can stir the Martinis. . . . In our opinion you will not need any cocktail spikes, or little jackets to tie around the base of glasses, or mittens to use shaking your shaker." They suggest the repertoire of any on-the-ball bachelorette should include the following popular cocktails: martini, manhattan, old-fashioned rye highball, Tom Collins, daiquiri, rum collins, and vermouth cassis. Very sound – although Hillis and Foltz's recommended martini will probably strike the modern reader as undrinkably wet. "Use two parts gin to one-half part French and one-half part Italian vermouth," they say. "Add a twist of lemon-peel and ice and stir (not shake) till really cold. Serve with a pitted, unstuffed olive in each glass. (There are innumerable variations of this recipe, but this one is a classic.)" To which we can only say: Yuck.

There is no entry here on the plain dry martini, actually, just because it is so ubiquitous. We have indicated preferences about spirits here and there, but there is no brand-whoring afoot and no discussion of finer examples of the respective genres, such as single-malt whisky (which does not belong in mixed drinks anyway). Our assumption on these points is that you will use whatever you prefer, or can afford. There are entries on about thirty drinks, the ones with the best literary and cinematic associations – the best stories. All of the drinks enjoy an established provenance: there are no newbies here, and no on-the-spot inventions of the kind that now crowd the hip lounges of our cities, their silly punning names presented in italic script and available for fifteen dollars a glass.

Inventing drinks is a game for fiction-writers and adolescents: just one of the commonalities between them. The late Douglas Adams, author of the *Hitchhiker's Guide to the Galaxy* series, gave us the Pan Galactic Gargle Blaster, for example, the undisputed "best drink in the universe." This drink is so good it produces an effect said to be similar to having a lemon wedge inserted in your brain. But invented drinks can also go badly wrong. In Anthony Powell's comic novel *From a View to a Death* (1933) – not a very comic title, admittedly – a young man called Torquil Fosdick, if you can believe that, bored of life in the English countryside, decides to throw a London-style cocktail party in the garden of the local pub, the Fox and Hounds. The guests include a half-dozen local youngsters, plus, acting as band, three wizened panhandlers, known as the Orphans, who play hand organs. "Will you have a martini or a fosdick," Torquil asks his dazed guests as they arrive all at once. "All of them chose a fosdick," the narrator notes, "Torquil's own concoction, which was sweet and evidently quite strong." We never learn what ingredients went into this mix, but we do know that the eldest of the Orphans, imbibing his rather too freely, makes a pass at Miss Gertrude Braby, the younger of the vicar's daughters. It all ends in tears, as indeed many a hopeful cocktail party is apt to do.

We realize it can be hard to resist the juvenile impulse to try new combinations of your favourite tipples ("Scotch and port? Hey, why not?") or just to mix whatever happens to be left in the liquor cabinet ("Hmm, Cointreau and Sambuca. I wonder . . ."). Together with some college friends of mine, I once upon a time helped invent three excellent drinks: (1) the *Psychedelic Wallflower*, despite its colourful name just Cointreau and tonic water over ice in a collins glass (and better than it sounds); (2) the *Cantini*, gin and vermouth poured into an army-surplus canteen and packed for a canoe trip; and (3) the *Poodle-on-a-Cloud*, a sort of margarita served with the glass embedded in a soup bowl filled with dry ice and a plastic poodle ornament. Obviously this last drink requires regular access to a chem lab, which suffices to reveal its essential nature as dopey kidstuff. There was also something we called the *Logical Positivist*, but nobody can now recall the relevant ingredients – or "truth conditions" as we liked to call them then. Ha ha.

There is no such newfangled nonsense in what follows, just solid contenders, some familiar and some less so but worth reviving. The drinks are defended, but this is not one of those reformist lifestyle books in the metrosexual mode of recent years. Really, there is no point to those books or television shows except a generalized disdain of unmarried heterosexual men, a desire to make all the world's straight bachelors look like feckless apes barely capable of shaving or dressing themselves, let alone cooking a balanced meal. Does anyone really need that? Who wants to be scolded about an alleged lack of sophistication under cover of cheerful flirting? Who wants to spend any time at all in the company of someone forever pulling style rank and wagging a (manicured) finger of disapproval?

Not us. The assumption in what follows is that the reader is just somebody who wants to know more about drinks – how to make them, and what they signify. We choose these drinks because they are both classic mixes and old favourites, but the choices are personal and sometimes perverse. There is no presumed argument about the necessary and sufficient features of a "classic." As Harold Bloom said about his picks for a literary survey called *Genius* (2002), "my choice is wholly arbitrary and idiosyncratic. These are certainly *not* 'the top one hundred,' in anyone's judgment, my own included. I wanted to write about these." Ditto.

Another writer, which is probably to say another drinker, might well have a very different list of classic cocktails. He or she might disagree with us about this detail or that. He or she might even suggest that we should drink a cosmopolitan. To this person we say: let a thousand mixes bloom. There is no room for acrimony in the brotherhood of the shaker.

Just don't – please, whatever they teach you in mixology school, do not – make a manhattan with bourbon.

GIMLET

They made an unlikely pair, the tough-guy private eye and the kept man from England slowly drinking himself to death in the harsh light of Southern California. Terry Lennox was the only friend Philip Marlowe ever got hooked on, a disfigured loser Marlowe liked in a world where nobody was nice enough to like.

In Raymond Chandler's *The Long Goodbye*, for no good reason he can see, Marlowe helps out the drunk, overdressed wastrel, and they become tight. Every month or so they meet and drink gimlets at Victor's, right after opening time, when, as Lennox says, "the air inside is cool and clean and everything is shiny and the barkeep is giving himself that last look in the mirror to see if his tie is straight and his hair is smooth."

Then there's murder, disappearance, more murder, and some beautiful women who can't be trusted. Also forgery, disguise, and more murder. The friendship doesn't last but the drink does, a tart aftertaste of male bonding. Once a year, Marlowe raises one to the memory of charming, doomed Lennox. The perfect drink for dark confidences, and their memory.

The gimlet can be abused all too easily, and in particular doesn't care for mixing. In Simon Raven's novel *Fielding Gray* (1967), an early entry in his salacious *roman-fleuve Alms for Oblivion* – a sort of poor man's cousin to Anthony Powell's *A Dance to the Music of Time* – the precocious schoolboys on the verge of great things celebrate the end of term with a drinks party. The three friends, Somerset Lloyd-James, Peter Morrison, and Fielding Gray, who will go in such different and unexpected directions, golden boy Gray in particular about to endure a fall, drink themselves into a tizzy. It is England in 1945, and they only have enough gin to make them think sherry is a good idea after a gimlet. Which is fine if the thing you want after the sherry is shameless homoerotic flirting followed by violent illness. Boys will have their fun.

Gimlets are simple and direct but, like all simple things, they have to be done right. "They don't know how to make them here," Lennox complains to Marlowe the first time they get drunk together. "What they call a gimlet is just some lime or lemon juice and gin with a dash of sugar and bitters. A real gimlet is half gin and half Rose's Lime Juice and nothing else. It beats martinis hollow."

That it does, but make it stronger and drier than that: combine two or even three parts gin to one part Rose's, shake hard with ice, and pour into a cocktail glass. You can have it over rocks if you like but that'll spoil that mouth-filling intensity, the sharp clear blow to the head. Avoid organic or local knock-off lime cordials, accept no garnishes. Steer clear of the high-end variations like vodka with Cointreau and lemon juice. No, no, no. Just cold gin and cold lime juice; a pal to clink with; secrets to share; nothing else. What else is there?

It's a good name, of piercing glances and precision-boring tools. It will, to be sure, make its sharp way into your brain and stay there. Be careful: the gimlet isn't overpowering, like a jet-fuel gin martini, but it can sneak up on you. "Alcohol is like love," Lennox says. "The first kiss is magic, the second is intimate, the third is routine. After that you take the girl's clothes off."

Yes. Your brother or friend along for the ride, stride into a dark bar in a wicked city, one of those red-banquette and dry-pretzel places where the barmen still wear jackets and, as though there was murder and betrayal and gunplay around your corners too, take a stool, take a pretzel, and say, looking the other way, "Gimme a gimlet, pal."

WHISKY SOUR

It's a grown-up drink, and frankly not all of them are despite the liquor laws. Sure, it probably takes a certain perverse courage for a middle-aged man to order, then publicly consume, a cosmopolitan. But it's not for you. The whisky sour is for you, when you are inking contracts, finalizing residuals, meeting your future father-in-law for the first time. It is the Deal-Sealer, the Bond, the Closer.

"Dexter King told me about running into my father, some years earlier, at the Downtown Association," a Louis Begley character says, "and how my father asked whether I was doing well. He is on the right track, Dexter replied, and I don't see what can derail him. Well, in law firm code language that means your boy will become partner as soon as his turn comes, and normally that makes the boy's father offer to buy you a whisky sour."

Exactly right. It is the drink of white-shoe lawyers everywhere, and you know without being told that "white-shoe," or just "shoe," is ancient Ivy League slang for top-drawer, first-rate, weenie-free. And if you don't know anybody called Dexter, follow the example of Calvin Trillin and invent an imaginary Yale College pal called, variously, Hatcher Baxter Thatcher, Thatcher Baxter Hatcher, and Hatcher Thatcher Baxter. Obviously it helps if you actually went to Yale, but it's not crucial. Just call whomever you're with "Baxter" or "Dexter" or both, and order yourselves a couple of whisky sours.

This is not Philip Marlowe's usual type of associate, nor his usual drink, but Marlowe quaffs a whisky or two at the beginning of Raymond Chandler's *Farewell, My Lovely* (1940) anyway. That's because his particular companion on that occasion is a certain Moose Maloy, a man "not more than six feet five inches tall and not wider than a beer truck." Moose is just out of the joint after eight long years for a murder he didn't do, and he's looking for his gal, Velma, who did. She's long gone, into another life entirely, but Moose doesn't know and doesn't care for the fact that her former nightclub hangout is now a gambling joint where white folks aren't welcome. Marlowe gets taken along for the ride just because he's that kind of nosey. He watches Moose make short work of the club's bouncer, throwing him across the room. "Some guys," he tells Marlowe, "has got wrong ideas about when to get tough." Marlowe is not about to disagree, over that or the choice of get-out-of-jail drink. "Whisky sour," the big man tells the petrified bartender. "Call yours," he tells Marlowe. "Whisky sour," Marlowe says. They have whisky sours.

That's just the beginning, and in the way of these things, at least in Chandler's rusted-out cityscape, celebration itself turns sour, there are more murders to come, and Velma turns out to be not what she seems. But there's other kinds of trouble in the offing too, because the whisky sour is among the most disputed mixes in the world of drink. Variations abound, not only on what counts as whisky, but with all kinds of exotic strangeness thrown in: Japanese plums, egg whites, 7-Up, orange juice, cherry juice, maple syrup. Egg whites! That's not a cocktail, it's a flip or a frappé or a nog. Maple syrup! What is this, brunch? There are also commercial "sour mixes" to be found on your grocer's shelves. Go there now and smash the bottles.

Always insist on the classic Closer, tart, sweet, and strong. This may involve a certain amount of trial and error, even a few tiresome arguments with bartenders when out on the town. Be firm, Baxter, firm; it's your drink.

First, two big jiggers of blended scotch. Respect yourself and pick a decent brand: Teacher's, Bell's, the Famous Grouse. Rye, you say? Sure, go ahead but that's a different drink: call it the Cranky Canuck. Bourbon is right out; just forget it. It's too sweet, it's made from corn mash, it's from the South: three sterling reasons to steer clear. Of course you could use Irish, but once you're there, why not just take the next logical step and drink the real thing?

Now add the juice of one lemon, one lime, a couple of teaspoons of fine sugar or plain syrup, a dash or two of bitters. Shake vigorously with cracked ice, strain, and serve. Use an old-fashioned glass or, if you have one, a sour glass – that little stemmed cylinder somewhere between a tumbler and a cocktail glass. Just a twist of lemon to garnish. No cherries, no orange slices, no umbrellas.

Like most drinks, and maybe even more than most, given its association with after-work celebration, the whisky sour should best be sampled around cocktail hour, which is to say sometime after 5 p.m. But there are exceptions, and one of them is the seasonal bachelor. In Billy Wilder's film *The Seven Year Itch* (1955), a transplanted stage comedy perhaps best remembered for Marilyn Monroe's iconic skirt-swirling cooldown over a Manhattan subway grate, Tom Ewell plays the hapless Mr. Sherman, a middle-management nebish left to his own devices when his wife flees town for the summer. His go-nowhere attempted seduction of Monroe, the hottie upstairs, was high hilarity in the mid-fifties, though it may strike more contemporary audiences as both goofy and inaccurate. (For one thing, it is much easier to get lucky in

Manhattan these days, even if you do happen to look like gawky, loose-jowled Tom Ewell.)

Be that as it may, Ewell's portrayal of the paradigmatic helpless male does generate one deathless drink-related line. A co-worker teases Sherman that, absent his wife, he must be, among other things, going without the most important meal of the day. "I had breakfast," Sherman replies indignantly. "A peanut-butter sandwich and two whisky sours."

Put 'er there, Dexter.

KIR ROYALE

D id you know that Michel de Montaigne, inventor of the modern essay, philosopher, and scholar, was mayor of Bordeaux for two terms? No, you didn't, because Montaigne never invented something really important, like a drink. Felix Kir, on the other hand, did exactly that while mayor of Dijon between 1945 and 1968. His favourite aperitif, a concoction of crisp white burgundy and local crème de cassis, proved so popular it soon acquired his name.

Plain kir is best served extremely cold, as wine writers like to say of poor vintages, or simply dumped over ice as a punch. Its refined royal cousin, on the other hand, may be consumed cool. Instead of still burgundy, add champagne to the blood-red cordial first macerated from blackcurrants by sixteenth-century French monks to combat the affliction of "wretchedness." There are other champagne mixes, peach-flavoured bellinis and strawberry this or that, not to mention the true champagne cocktail, with a lump of sugar soaked in brandy then brimmed with bubbly, which is what Victor Laszlo orders for himself and Ilsa at Rick's Café Americain in *Casablanca* (1942). But the kir royale is the best of them, silky perfection in a glass.

It's a date drink, a romancer, the epitome of smart sipping before dinner. Always order two, because you only ever drink it when sidling up to the bar with that swell girl on your arm. You know the one: the one who flirted with you across the room, then gave you her number on a paper napkin marked with lipstick. The one who laughs at all your jokes, strokes the arm of your suit, and draws every eye in the room. Sure, she's trouble. But sometimes trouble is what you want.

And of course it doesn't have to be a girl. In Bret Easton Ellis's *The Rules of Attraction*, young Paul Denton, *Fountainhead*-reading Bennington undergraduate, comes to Boston for dinner with his mother at the Ritz-Carlton. Also there, her best friend, Mrs. Jared, and *her* son, Richard – Paul's high-school crush, fresh back from Sarah Lawrence, now decked out in Wayfarers, platinum blond buzzcut, and Bronski Beat accessories. They are sitting in the plush, overheated hotel bar, the "elegant, tacky, big cave," all four of them, mothers and sons together. Richard has already killed a bottle of Jack Daniels. "He looks, unfortunately, pretty hot," Paul muses. "He sits across from me, making lewd gestures that I pray neither mother will notice. His foot is now in my crotch but I'm too nervous to get hard."

Well, who hasn't been *there*? "He's drinking champagne Kirs and he's downed about four," Paul continues, "all of them carefully and with what looks to me a definite sense of purpose." And what better way to drink them. But four is too many, especially after whisky.

Richard makes a noisy exit, it's all so embarrassing, but later, Paul's mother takes him back down to the bar for a quiet chat. She orders two more. "I focused all my attention on the way the waiter quickly, numbly opened each small bottle of Taittinger and poured them into tall thin glasses," she says. "And how very beautiful it looked when the champagne slowly dissolved the reddish purple cassis at the bottom of each glass." Wistfully, she tells Paul that she and his father had come there seventeen years before for their fifth wedding anniversary. "It was in December and it was snowing and we would order these." This is what she wants to tell him: they are getting divorced.

People used to pre-dinner drinks of tougher disposition may find kir royale sickly and effete. Too much cassis is the usual culprit. There are recipes that call for five parts champagne to one of cassis, which is just sick, and heavy-handed bartenders may offer you a gaggy stew the colour of cherry cola. Send it back and insist on wielding the cassis bottle yourself. About nine parts champagne to one part cassis is what you're after. The cassis should turn the gold wine palest rose, kissing the sparkle with a grace note of colour and taste. You want to taste the champagne as it acquires new texture, not witness its murder by blackcurrants. Your barman may attempt to toss a twist of lemon or even a couple of stray raspberries into your glass. Hold up a firm hand and forbid this.

Dispute rages over whether to pour the cassis or the champagne first. Top-down cassis will ensure the drink is properly mixed, because the heavier cordial will dilute evenly downwards, and that is good form. But bottom-up cassis means the dark red potion will pool in the bottom of your flute like a miniature sunset backlit by bubbles, and that is cool. As you're drinking, feel free to explain the physics of fluid dispersion to your date. She's not listening now anyway; she's flirting with someone else across the room. Kiss her on the cheek, pat your wallet, and order two more.

Resist the temptation to substitute inferior sparkling wine for champagne. There's no need to insist on original Cassis de Dijon, but don't slosh cheap Spanish cava or Italian Prosecco over cassis. Peachy Prosecco, especially, has no business acquiring any new flavours or sugar content. Biscuity Veuve Clicquot is excellent; or, even better, one of those stern Heidsiecks, where the wine seems almost to vaporize on your tongue. Cassis will tame that, bring it sweetly to earth.

Is she still by your side? Yes? Then it's time for dinner.

TOM COLLINS

Ernie Cholakis – star running back on the varsity football
team, flawless profile, bags of charm – where is he now?
Stole your date on prom night way back in 1980, maybe even
had his way with her somewhere in the cavernous hotel
complex where you all were, besuited and scrubbed and
freshly shaved, restless for what the world had to offer. Where
is he now?

You didn't care then and you don't care now. She was
somebody's sister's cousin's best friend's niece, and the best
thing you can say for her is that she was game to drive up from
North Dakota or wherever the hell it was to be some Catholic
schoolboy's blind prom date, and you kind of hope she and

Ernie had a good time, wherever they were, whatever they were doing. You – you were on the dancefloor, and at the bar, and then on the dancefloor again, and while the other guys were breaking up with their dates so they could go to some local college with no strings attached, you were drinking Tom Collinses and thinking, like Richard Dreyfus in *American Graffiti*, that you were blowing that particular popsicle stand any minute and heading east for university and that, yes, Tom Collins is, in fact, the best drink around when you're standing there, leaning against the bar in a tan summerweight suit, watching the football team get stupid on beer.

Who was Tom Collins? People say the bartender, or maybe the client, or maybe just the "Old Tom" sweet gin used in the original drink. Does it really matter, any more than it matters where Ernie Cholakis is now? Tom Collins gave his name to this unimprovable long drink and that is enough. There is a seat in heaven reserved for him, just as there is a circle in hell reserved for arrogant jocks with movie-star good looks who peaked in high school and thought it was okay to steal another guy's date. Fearful symmetry, as the man said.

It starts with gin, always gin, though you can waste time fiddling with such lesser Collins siblings as John (whisky), Pedro (rum), Ivan (vodka), Mike (Irish whisky), Jack (apple jack), and even Brandy (well, brandy). If, for reasons that passeth understanding, you don't like gin, we are at a loss. Aggressive vodka marketing makes people think Baltic potato moonshine can replace gin in any drink, and if that's your inclination we can't stop you. But just a word of suggestion: any mix that tastes good with vodka tastes better with gin. Try it and see. And where better to start than with a genuine Tom Collins, tall, smooth, and cool, the most fun gin ever had in a straight-sided glass.

As you'd expect, there are sugary Collins mixes for sale in grocery stores – ignore them. Just pour two jiggers of good gin into a shaker with some cracked iced, the juice of one lemon, and a spoonful of superfine sugar. Shake, then strain into a frosted collins glass, or any tall glass, filled with ice cubes. Top up with a couple of glugs of club soda, for fizz. No 7-Up, please. You can toss on a flag garnish – a slice of orange (East Coast) or lime (West Coast) skewered by a maraschino cherry – but that's just for girls and holidays. Drink immediately but not quickly.

We know, we know: there are gin-and-tonic purists out there who will say, why mess with such a clearly good thing? Surely (they want to say), the g-and-t is as good as it gets when it comes to mixing gin with anything, the platonic form of the mixed drink. And up to a point they are right, especially if the gin and tonic are in roughly equal proportion, there's a fresh lime wedge squeezed on top, and you have a bowl of those little goldfish crackers ready to hand. Yes.

But the Tom Collins adds jaunty refinement to that experience; it makes a very good thing even better. In fact, think of it as the g-and-t's older brother. Let's call him Tommy. The one with the good record collection and long-haired, college-age girlfriend. The one who knows that if his date wanders off with a football player, she'll be back eventually. Or not. Who knows that cool is as cool does. Who's just, you know, hanging out here at the bar, thinking about maybe dancing when he finishes his drink, thinking about life in general, thinking about thinking. Or not.

The Brooklyn

Uncle Manhattan

The Bronx

MANHATTAN

"Give me women! give me comrades and lovers by the thousand! /Let me see new ones every day! let me hold new ones by the hand every day! /Give me such shows! give me the streets of Manhattan!"

So said Walt Whitman, and absolutely, yes, the streets and the women and the lovers, bring them on. But here's an even better idea: just give us the manhattan, cold and dusky in a frosted glass, the luxurious swirl of rye and vermouth, a dash of Angostura bitters for tone, the one and only cocktail that really demands a cherry.

After all, the cherry is the red orb of the sun, isn't it, glowing in an amber sky over New Jersey, a sky murky from the light-bending pollution, the Hudson-borne toxins and particles and motes. Make sure the barman shakes your manhattan hard, so that platelets of ice float on top. Drink it at the bar, by yourself, thinking deep, bustling, gridlocked thoughts.

It is a big-city name for a big-city drink; like the town itself, a manhattan demands your full attention. Whitman again: "– Give me the shores and wharves heavy-fringed with black ships! /O such for me! O an intense life, full to repletion and varied! /The life of the theatre, bar-room, huge hotel, for me!" Yes. Or just say, as Fat Tony and his Springfield henchmen do when moonlighting Bart Simpson mixes them a perfect example, "Supoib."

The Savoy Cocktail Book, that indispensable comprehensive guide, suggests two parts Canadian Club to one part Italian vermouth, and a dash of bitters; shake with cracked ice, strain, and add the cherry. Experiment with the proportions – that's old-school mixology and therefore probably too sweet. The Savoyards also gently explain the manhattan by saying it is "named for the island on which the city of New York stands," which will come as news to Brooklynites and Bronxers.

Those charming boroughs, as it happens, have their own, lesser-known cocktails. The Brooklyn, befitting a once-poor niece to rich uncle Manhattan, now hipper than the island itself, is a variation on a theme. Mix two parts C.C. with one part French vermouth, add a dash of maraschino liqueur and a dash of Amer Picon, stir, and strain. No cherry, because this is drier – and indeed the so-called dry manhattan, made with French instead of Italian vermouth, or a mixture of the two, is really a Brooklyn. But don't expect many barkeeps to know that.

The Bronx, up on the unruly roof of Manhattan, is something else again, half dry gin and half a swirl of French vermouth, Italian vermouth, and orange juice. Tasty, and more sophisticated than Bronx cheers and Bronx Bombers would have you believe. Alec Connage, a Princeton classmate of feckless Amory Blaine in F. Scott Fitzgerald's *This Side of Paradise* (1920), knows what he's about when he leads a gaggle of the overprivileged boys on a dine-and-dash tour of the Jersey Shore. "Eight Bronxes," he commands the dim waiter at lunch, "and a Club Sandwich and Juliennes. Food for one. Hand the rest around." The resulting bill – $8.25 in 1920s-era money – does not, needless to say, get fully settled.

Ah, the arrogance of Youth, especially at Princeton – or the English seaside. In Elizabeth Bowen's novel *The Death of the Heart* (1938), a teenaged orphan, Portia, is sent by "her people" – an older half-brother and his wife – to spend the winter season in the coastal town of Seale. There she meets and soon runs with a rather fast set, including a rogue army officer called Bursley and the caddish Eddie, a quicksilver charmer she knows from London, rather improperly installed as a guest in the same house as she. There is hand-holding, snogging, and even – wait for it – some light petting. *Shockage!*

One memorable evening the whole crew visits a kitschy seaside pleasure dome for drinks and *conversazione*.

"Indoors, among the mirrors and pillars, they found Mr. Bursley and Daphne, cozy over a drink. Reproaches and rather snooty laughs were exchanged, then Mr. Bursley, summoning the waiter, did what was right by everyone. Clara and Portia were given orangeade, with hygienic straws twisted up in paper; Daphne had another bronx, Evelyn a side-car. The men drank whisky – with the exception of Eddie, who asked for a double gin with a dash of Angostura: this he insisted in dashing in himself, and so much fuss had seldom been made before." That will be a pink gin, of course, and Eddie has another too – this time putting in too much Angostura and so having to add more gin. Daphne, meanwhile, she of the second Bronx, "looked flushed and pleased."

That state, alas, does not last. While Eddie tickles Clara with a straw paper and Mr. Bursley does an imitation of Donald Duck, Daphne knocks over her third Bronx. Her comb gets stolen, someone named Cecil gets sick, and funboy Eddie gets a drunken attack of remorse, finishing the evening sobbing on the balcony as Portia silently looks on.

So the Bronx, not to mention the pink gin, bears watching too. There is a family of Bronx variations for the adventurous (or those with a more level head): the Bronx Silver (add an egg white), the Bronx Terrace (step up the gin; lime instead of orange juice – a quasi-gimlet), and the Crystal

Bronx (hold the gin, add soda). There's even such a thing as a Knickerbocker, with one-third French vermouth and a dash of Italian, twist – a very wet martini.

Indeed, not surprisingly, New York–themed cocktails go forth and multiply with some volume. We will mention just two more, both variations on reliable themes. The New York Sour is pretty much what its name suggests, a whisky sour with bells on. Four parts blended whisky, scotch for preference this time, join three parts fresh lemon juice and a teaspoon of bar sugar. Shake with ice and strain into a chilled sour glass. Then – the Midtown flourish – float a tablespoon of dry red wine on top. Not for everyone, mixing grain and grape like that, but worth a try. The New Yorker Cocktail, rather strangely for anything associated with the Big Apple, goes largely unappreciated: people don't order or mix it nearly enough. Combine four parts blended whisky with two parts fresh lemon juice, a teaspoon of simple syrup, and a half-teaspoon grenadine. Shake with cracked ice, strain into a chilled cocktail glass, and garnish with a lemon twist. Hard to describe, but extremely well balanced if you like scotch.

But why not just stick to the manhattan, and to reliable Canadian whisky? Pushy bartenders may offer to make you a "bourbon manhattan," and, while not unpleasant, this is not correct. Call it an Atlanta or a Charlotte or a . . . you know what? Who really cares. Call it whatever you want. Have a manhattan instead, and tell the dude C.C. or Seagram's, and no fussing. As Homer Simpson notes while desperately navigating the concrete canyons of Capital City, we crave familiar things when trapped in the "urban death-maze" of the big metrop.

A manhattan consumed in Manhattan has a straight-up neatness – even if sometimes also an overtone of melancholy, especially if one is alone. In Dawn Powell's novel of New York arty types falling for Midwestern businessmen, *Angels on Toast* (1940), a young commercial artist named Ebie reflects on her possible solitary future as she watches elderly lady residents move through a shabby Gramercy hotel one sad Sunday afternoon. These forgotten suffragettes, once-celebrated authors, and former marquee stars, were, Ebie notes, "without too much obvious haste taking their places in the grill-room, nodding and smiling to the waitresses, carrying their knitting and a slender volume of some English bard, anything to prop up against their first Manhattan." Shudder.

The scotch alternative to the manhattan has a more considerable pedigree, being, of course, the Rob Roy, a fine cocktail favoured in officers' messes, hotel lounges, railway-terminal bars, and other places where small-time intrigue and hard drinking go hand in hand. The standard Rob Roy calls for equal parts scotch and Italian vermouth, plus the dash of bitters, but that's a lot of vermouth. More scotch, please, and give it a good old shake before you pour the brave laddie out. Add a cherry for swagger.

Okay, one more twist before we leave the Highlands and return to the high-rises: the delicious Rabbie Burns Cocktail (incorrectly labelled the "Bobby Burns" in the *Savoy* guide). This Rob Roy relative calls for equal parts scotch and Italian vermouth, plus three rich dashes of Benedictine. Shake, strain, serve with twist. The result is pretty swanky, especially considering it is named for a rural versifier of uncertain talent and morals. "One of the very best Whisky Cocktails," the *Savoy* experts note. "A very fast mover on Saint Andrew's Day." (Which, if you didn't know, is November 30 and worth celebrating the next time it comes around.) But, Scottish or not, think about whipping up a batch of these on Burns Day, January 25, to chase the haggis.

But O! Give us a manhattan instead! Million-footed manhattan! Superb-faced manhattan! A last word from Walt, the man, the singer, lusty dweller and walker in the city of cities, the bard of intoxication. "Stand up, tall masts of Mannahatta! stand up, beautiful hills of Brooklyn! . . . Sound out, voices of young men! loudly and musically call me by my nighest name!"

Call us too, Walt – and if you stand up to the bar first, order us one, icy, sweet, and straight-up.

ZOMBIE

In George Romero's film *Dawn of the Dead* (1979), which everyone knows was the apocalypti-kitsch sequel to *Night of the Living Dead* (1968), crazed zombies – the stalking, moaning, flesh-munching undead – infiltrate a barricaded shopping mall, tumbling down escalators and staggering blindly into display racks and glass storefronts, at once pathetic and apathetic. You have to admit, hell of a name for a drink.

The *Oxford English Dictionary* says the word *zombie* is "of obscure West African origin," but others say it's just the Kongo word for "fetish." The drink's origin is similarly disputed. While absent from the standard mixological treatises of the 1930s, it was featured prominently as a novel tipple at the

1939 World's Fair in New York, and well known to post-Eisenhower cultural life, along with other suburban *Mad Magazine* mixes like the Harvey Wallbanger and the stinger.

Ah, the stinger – the cocktail Grace Kelly's Tracy Lord uses to combat a hangover after her ill-advised drinking binge with visiting journalist Frank Sinatra in *High Society* (1956), the musical version of George Cukor's *The Philadelphia Story* (1940), which features Katharine Hepburn in a far superior turn as the wilful heiress about to wed stodgy dolt after ditching more exciting soulmate. (In the earlier effort, James Stewart has the Sinatra role, and Cary Grant plays the ex, C.K. Dexter Haven. Maybe all you need to know about the shift from major to minor is that Bing Crosby, of all people, has the Grant role in the musical.) Anyway, *High Society* is nobody's idea of a great movie but it delivers some decent tunes and manages, somehow, to be a movie with a quiver of great scenes. Like Kelly, at the height of her icy beauty, that perfect nose, those long gorgeous legs, playing with a toy model of the yacht *True Love* in the backyard pool of her Newport mansion. Or her again, trying to remember just what happened the night before with the charming journalist. The morning-after stinger doesn't help Tracy's memory any more than it will help yours in similar circumstances, but it is certainly one way to get yourself back into tone after a rough night of too much fizzy wine.

The stinger does not enjoy the cultural-wallpaper ubiquity of the martini (a drink so pervasive it needs no entry in this book – but see the gibson); nevertheless, once upon a time, it was a swanky tipple of choice and has the impressive cinematic presence to prove it.

In Billy Wilder's *The Apartment* (1960), dopey insurance clerk C.C. Baxter, played with nasal fussiness by Jack Lemmon, is regularly ousted from his West Sixties Manhattan flat so that junior executives can have it off with their floozies. Eventually senior executive Jeff D. Sheldrake, a smarmy Fred MacMurray, will outrank them all, taking sassy young elevator girl Miss Kubelik (Shirley MacLaine) for a rough ride. That's when the film moves from comedy to drama, and so to greatness. Mr. Dobisch, from administration, kicking Baxter out of his place late one evening, pleads over the phone that he is getting lucky with a Marilyn Monroe lookalike. (She sounds like her too.) The amorous pair arrive by taxi, drinks from the last bar still in hand. "Watch those stingers, baby," Dobisch says as they lurch up the brownstone steps.

The stinger is also what Cary Grant, as the suave angel Dudley in *The Bishop's Wife* (1947), orders to placate three judgmental parish matrons who see him lunching intimately with, well, the bishop's wife. That would be Loretta Young, the bishop himself being David Niven, of course. "Michel, bring us three Benedictines," Cary tells the owner as he coaxes the disapproving ladies over to their table. Then he takes a closer look at their thin-lipped, sex-starved faces. "Make that three stingers."

In *The Big Clock* (also 1947), Ray Milland is an over-worked crime-magazine publisher called Stroud. Late for a lunch meeting with his wife, he is drinking at the bar of the Van Barth Hotel in New York. As he orders two more stingers for himself and an associate, Rita Johnson, the disgruntled mistress of his boss, joins them at the bar. "Do you always drink stingers, Mr. Stroud?" How does she know his name? Because she's already planning to use him as a way of getting back the boss, Charles Laughton, who wants to throw her over. Actually, though neither of the two drinkers knows it, he wants to kill her and frame up Stroud for the murder. Ouch.

Before that happens, Stroud will move on to champagne with lunch, make some extravagant promises, and then get fired. Then things start to get really bad. (Stingers and champagne: not a recommended midday combination.) Later the same day, briefly back in the Van Barth bar, and now minus wife but plus Rita Johnson – we know, we know, these old film noir plots can twist the melon; you'll just have to see the movie – he decides to return to the scene of the cocktail crime, albeit with a twist. "Bartender, bring us two more stingers," he commands. "And this time make them with green mint." "Green mint?" says the appalled barman. "Oh no."

"I tell you," the barman says later to the cops, when Milland is being pursued for a murder he didn't commit, "that was the most horrible drink I had in my life." Yeah, and look what happened to the guy who ordered them. Well, he gets Stroud off in the end, and even gets the wife back onside, but not without some considerable thrills and difficulty. Rita Johnson alas stays dead. So stick to the original article. That's four parts brandy plus two parts white crème de menthe, shaken hard with cracked ice and poured into a chilled cocktail or old-fashioned glass. Stings all right . . .

The only other drink that regularly features as a reliable hangover cure, as noted, is the Corpse Reviver – probably a legacy of its colourful name. It actually comes in two varieties that are in fact completely different drinks. The Corpse Reviver No. 1 combines four parts apple brandy with two parts regular brandy and one part sweet vermouth. All of that is shaken hard with ice and strained into a chilled cocktail glass. The Corpse Reviver No. 2 is better, if only because gin is less likely to kill you than brandy in the long run. It combines two parts each of dry gin, Cointreau, Kina Lillet, and fresh lemon juice with a dash of absinthe or Pernod. Shake well with cracked ice and strain into a cocktail glass. *The Savoy Cocktail Book* points out the perhaps obvious irony that "Four of these taken in swift succession will unrevive the corpse again." Cure, as so often, turns to curse.

Speaking of revived corpses, let's go back to the zombie. So maybe it was the war, maybe creole jazz, maybe nothing in particular, but by the time Roger Moore was rogering Solitaire in 1973, the zombie was a standard fixture in fern bars, breezeway patios, and shag-carpeted rec rooms throughout the land. You can see why. It's a punch that packs a punch, easy to drink but efficiently designed to make you paralytic, half dead, not quite here.

"A back-alley neon sign, the first I'd seen, / drew us sweetly down and in to brightness," writes Lavinia Greenlaw in her poem "Zombies": "a doll's parasol, a spike of green cherries, / the physic of apricot brandy, actual limes / and morning-to-night shades of rum." It gets a bit messy afterwards, as will happen with the zombie: "[S]triking out once across ploughed and frozen earth," the poem continues, "lurching from rut to rut until at the edge / we smashed our way out through a hedge, to fall / eight feet to the road. Of course, we felt nothing." Of course.

The simplicity of the basic zombie recipe masks a multitude of possible sins, however. Stranded one New Year's Eve in North Bay, Ontario, nobody's idea of a swish cocktail town, you might find yourself asking for a zombie in the nearly deserted function room of the chilly Ramada Inn, noting the heavy Supertramp presence in the DJ's repertoire and wondering whether to kill yourself then or later, only to be served a frothy crimson drink concocted of equal parts

Captain Morgan white, Hawaiian Punch red, and ketchup. You might also find yourself sliding by degrees into a living-dead condition where zombies lead to other venomous mixes. Richard Tull, the hapless protagonist of Martin Amis's *The Information* (1995), is given to gloomy zombie ingestion at his local, the Canal Creperie – "the resort of insomniac boozers prepared to pay for, and sit quite near to, the platefuls of food which the law obliged them to order with their drinks." Richard is the gamely, lamely toiling writer of "serious" fiction whose unpublished novel is known to give readers debilitating, possibly fatal, migraines. Meanwhile, his glib and semi-talented friend Glyn Barry has gone global with a bestseller stuffed with facile humanist claptrap. Richard has lots to drink about.

"He waved to the waitress. No, not another Zombie, thank you; he would try a Tarantula." Later: "He waved to the waitress. No, not another Tarantula, thank you; he would try a Rattlesnake."

Though no real-world referent can be found for the Tarantula, there is, in fact, a drink called the Rattlesnake. It's no picnic. Combine four parts blended whisky with one part fresh lemon juice, a teaspoon of simple syrup, a quarter teaspoon of Pernod, and the white of one egg. Shake all ingredients with cracked ice and pour over ice cubes in a chilled old-fashioned glass.

Any cocktail using egg whites seems a little off to this book, so we will stick with the zombie. The key is good rum, and lots of it. There should be three ounces, one each of light, dark, and amber. Use Bacardi. In general, rum is a crude spirit, a sailor's cheap stone, one small step away from the spit-and-rot sugar fermentations of anthropological interest. And there is surely no excuse for the rum-and-Coke except to get teenagers drunk. But the Cuba Libre, the elegant version thereof, is not without merit; and a well-made zombie can almost make rum sophisticated.

Then add juice. This may vary a little but it should always include fresh limes and something tropical, pineapple or papaya or mango. The catalytic glug of apricot brandy or cherry whisky is a matter of taste, but creates a smooth finish, the way a knob of butter adds lustre to an already-rich sauce. Some people splash in a little Triple Sec too, but now you're just talking crazy. Shake hard and pour over ice in a chilled collins or highball glass. Add a cherry or a flag, powdered sugar on the rim, and even a parasol if you're feeling cheeky. Then, finally, float a teaspoon of 151-proof rum on top. Resist the impulse to set this rum-based bomb alight and just drink it. Slowly.

It's a bright drink with an evil centre, earning its underworldly name and fearsome reputation. It will flatter you with good cheer and then, if you are not vigilant, bring you low with a host of curses. One minute you're tossing them back like Kool-Aid, the next you're wondering if Jim Jones is the bartender. Like those dry-ice-and-flame Trader Vic's concoctions of which it is the precursor – the Borneo Fog-Cutter, the Polynesian Torch-Bearer – the zombie is made for dark corners and dark feelings. The Fog-Cutter doesn't cut fog so much as create it. Consider: four parts light rum, two parts gin, two parts brandy, three parts fresh lemon, and two parts fresh orange juice, and a teaspoon of almond syrup. Mix all together and shake with ice. Pour over ice cubes in a collins glass – and then float a dollop of sweet sherry on top.

Like that massive mix, the zombie will teach you a thing or two about being undead. "Was it not ourselves who frightened us most?" Greenlaw's narrator asks. "As if brightness or sweetness could save us." As if.

NEGRONI

If you can believe Warren Beatty as an Italian gigolo, as opposed to the Californian one he played in *Shampoo* (1975), then you'll go for *The Roman Spring of Mrs. Stone*, a sexy 1961 potboiler based on Tennessee Williams's only novel. The Mrs. Stone in question, played by Vivien Leigh, is an aging Broadway star who, having recently flopped as Juliet, goes to Rome for solace. Her husband promptly dies, leaving her rich and ripe for a scheming Contessa (Lotte Lenya), who feeds her to the handsome cad Conte Paolo di Leo – Beatty. He seduces her hard before hitting her even harder for money. It all ends badly, as these things will. There is a 2002 remake starring Helen Mirren, Anne Bancroft, and cheesy Olivier Martinez, but hold out for the original.

Hold out, too, for the negroni, the gin and Campari cocktail that, along with Rome itself, is an uncredited star. Williams, longtime visitor to Italy, was a dedicated chronicler of dissipation, a man who knew his drinks and drunks. The negroni is a deceptively elegant ruby-coloured slammer, aromatic, bright, and clean-tasting. It is resonant of outdoor cafés and reclining dolce-vita evenings; it will, like a gorgeous but wicked lover, drain your resistance, then exhaust your bank account and autopsy your heart. Avanti!

It's not for fence-sitters. Some people love its astringent bittersweet chill so much they'll drink nothing else, no matter the location or time of year; others find it harsh, lip-puckering, about as palatable as cherry-flavoured Vicks expectorant. One legend of the drink is that it makes you decisive, and first-timers may find it makes them decide never to order one again. The reason is Campari, the medicinal Italian aperitif allegedly concocted in the 1850s by a precocious mixmaster of genius, Gaspare Campari, who ruled the Bass Bar in Turin from the age of fourteen. Campari is an acquired taste not everyone acquires, like Schoenberg or Pynchon – or Warren Beatty. It's flavoured by a secret blend of natural herbs and spices, with some tree bark and citrus peel thrown in; the result is a bright red chemical solution, bitter as hell, whose famous bottle and café umbrellas are instant metonyms of elegant Mediterranean leisure. Mixed with soda or orange juice, with lots of ice and maybe a teaspoon of fine sugar, it will put a sharp little zing into your brunch or picnic.

The negroni, meanwhile, is probably best consumed only after all thoughts of productivity or sanity have been abandoned for the day. The classic article is a symphony of thirds, with equal parts gin, Campari, and sweet vermouth, shaken hard in cracked ice, strained, and served up in a cocktail glass. Something like one and a half ounces of each should do, but instead of fussing with finicky measures, why not slosh big amounts into your shaker and pour out a few cold ones as demand dictates. If you like one negroni, you'll certainly like another. And don't listen to people who would serve it on the rocks, or who say stirred not shaken. There should be a miniature ice floe in your martini glass, like a tiny tasty pond breaking up at the first spring thaw.

Traditional garnish is an orange wheel or twist, plus a coating of sugar on the rim – an option not really worth adding unless you're worried about the medicinal bite of the Campari, in which case why bother with the drink at all? You can use vodka in place of gin, but that would be more ill-advised than usual, since it lacks the oily aromatic sweetness needed to balance the Campari. Likewise if you choose dry vermouth over sweet, a move that will result in a drink so tart it makes your teeth quiver. Some modern bartenders vary the proportions – three parts gin, two Campari, one vermouth (the Rocket Negroni – 3, 2, 1!); or 35%, 35%, 30% (the Rocket Science Negroni – too much math).

Legend says the cocktail was invented by a customer, not a bartender. Count Camillo Negroni, a high-living Florentine aristocrat of the 1920s, perhaps nursing a hangover or trying to impress a wealthy American lady friend, asked for a slurp of gin to be added to the standard Americano aperitif of Campari and vermouth. He liked the result so much he ordered it again and again until the waiters of Florence gave him eponymous credit. Other stories say an expatriate American martini drinker, looking for novelty, asked for a straight-up gin and Campari mix, which the sensitive Italians then softened with vermouth. Either way, the negroni is clearly, like pepperoni pizza and Francis Ford Coppola, the result of brilliant Italian-American negotiation. After two of them you might even begin to appreciate Warren Beatty's Italian accent.

Well, maybe three.

GIBSON

So there you are, minding your own business in the Oak Room Bar, a happy-go-lucky Madison Avenue adman, suave and cynical, when one of those little mistakes settles around you like a noose. You make for the phone just as someone announces a call for George Kaplan.

But the thing is this: there are goons in the bar waiting for Kaplan. Your name is Thornhill, not Kaplan, but now that it looks as though you're taking the call, do you really think the goons will believe you? No. Kaplan doesn't exist, but you don't know that yet; neither do the goons. There's some stolen microfilm involved, a defection, treason, the CIA, a sultry blonde double-agent, a murderous crop-duster, and a scramble across Washington's nose. Madness, as Hamlet and Hitchcock said, runs *north by northwest*.

But first they try to kill you with drink out on Long Island. Then they kill another guy while you happen to be standing next to him, and you pull the knife out of his back. Bad day. Bang goes a flashbulb. Instant fugitive. You flee to Grand Central Terminal – because where else? – and sneak aboard the Twentieth Century to Chicago wearing yesterday's suit and your cool outsized sunglasses.

And there she is: Eva Marie Saint, cool and collected, hair a lustrous white-gold helmet, mouth at once serious and luscious, all alone in the dining car. Her name, it will turn out, is Eve Kendall. You sit down across from her – she's arranged it, in fact – shades still on, light her cigarette, and order yourself a gibson.

Good call. Nothing clears the mind of a man on the run better than a gelid shot of nearly straight gin backed with a single cocktail onion. The gibson is as close to zero-degree drinking as it is humanly possible to come: see-through, smart, drained of colour. The first sip should taste like a knife to the head, a clean incision that lets in air and makes your thoughts instantly lucid. This won't last, so enjoy it while it does and try to make any important decisions, like where you're going to spend the night, right now.

Just another name for a martini, you say, but no. Old-time gibsons were half gin and half French vermouth, but the

up-to-date article should be drier than the dustiest martini –
a few dashes of vermouth at most, maybe even the proverbial
bottle opened briefly on the other side of the room. The onion,
meanwhile, takes a swanky step beyond common lemon twist
or green olive. No brine and no citrus, the onion is sharp,
alien, uncompromising. It sounds a tiny call to arms, a miniature tastebud clarion.

A different man, a different train, but still Madison Avenue
because where else? In "The Five-Forty-Eight," adman Blake
has slept with his secretary, then had her fired, because he's
just the sort of heartless cad you find in a lot of John Cheever's
stories. Now the girl is after him. Yes, it's six months later and
she's *stalking* Blake down the streets of Manhattan. He ducks
into a men's bar. Another fugitive, another girl, another kind
of crime.

"He ordered a gibson and shouldered his way in between
two other men at the bar, so that if she should be watching
from the window she would lose sight of him. The place was
crowded with commuters putting down a drink before the
ride home. . . . Blake began to relax as soon as he tasted his
gibson and looked around at the common, mostly not-young
faces that surrounded him and that were worried, if they were
worried at all, about tax rates and who would be put in charge
of merchandising. He tried to remember her name – Miss
Dent, Miss Bent, Miss Lent – and he was surprised to find
that he could not."

Blake drinks a second gibson and so misses the express train to Westchester, catching the 5:48 local instead. Uh-oh. The girl is on it, and she has a gun. Should have made it just one drink, my friend.

What is it about gibsons and cads? In *The Best of Everything*, April Morrison falls for handsome charmer Dexter Key, that smooth-talking narcissus who strings her along for months, feeding a fantasy that they will one day get married. April discovers the truth only when she calls Dexter's mother and is treated like a distant acquaintance. That night, at his swell apartment, Dexter says, "Hey, let's have Gibsons tonight instead of Martinis, I bought some onions." April presses him about their "engagement"; why was his mother so distant to her future daughter-in-law? "Dexter held the Gibson very carefully so that it would not spill over the brim and took a sip at it. He seemed much more interested in the mechanics of the glass and liquid than the situation called for." Oops: danger, danger, April Morrison! The boom is lowering!

It ends happily enough for April, but not before heartbreak and an illegal abortion. And, per the noted wisdom of Tom Wolfe, that nobody can find true love in New York, she has to return home to Colorado to find marital peace – not with Dexter, it hardly needs adding.

What is it about gibsons and crime? Both Philip Marlowe, Raymond Chandler's detective, and Lew Archer, the creation of Ross MacDonald, seem to favour it while on the job. In

The Galton Case (1959), Archer is having lunch with a doctor who is worried his daughter has been charmed by an heir who may really be an imposter and a hood. The doc orders a gibson and Archer takes one too. "As a medical man," he says, "I feel it's my duty to perpetuate the little saving vices. It's probably safer to overdrink than it is to overeat."

Well, maybe. Marlowe, in Chandler's *Playback* (1958), is tailing a girl who had earlier, for no clear reason, hit him on the head with a whisky bottle. He finds her in a dim night-club where "half a dozen couples were throwing themselves around with the reckless abandon of a night watchman with arthritis." Marlowe sits at the bar. "I ordered a double Gibson and asked if I could have a club sandwich where I was." Later: "The Gibson arrived. I could make out the shape of the glass and there seemed to be something in it. I tasted it and it wasn't too bad." Unfortunately, that's the high point of an evening where at least one person is going to end up dead.

Not all fugitives risk death and not all of them flee crimes, even imaginary or moral ones. In *All About Eve* (1950), just before uttering the deathless line about fastening your seat-belts, Margo Channing (Bette Davis) asks her playwright boyfriend for "a martini, very dry," an order echoed, naturally, by creepy Eve (Anne Baxter). When the drinks arrive, Eve is absent and the boyfriend hands hers over to best friend Karen, saying, "You look like a gibson girl." At this point it's hard to tell if the drink contains an olive or an onion, that is, whether the slightly distracted boyfriend got the order wrong or is just turning a phrase. What we do know is that Margo downs hers in one and mounts the stairs with a doomed, defiant look. You can feel her happy youth disappearing almost as fast as the drink. It's going to be a bumpy night!

From Eve, the first criminal, to Poppy. Poppy Minkel is running from dreary respectability in Laurie Graham's novel *The Unfortunates* (2003). Daughter of a mustard fortune, apparently destined for Upper West Side death by boredom, she bolts. Over and over, as it will turn out. But the first time, she simply moves out and sets herself up as a lady-about-town in 1930s New York. "I decided on a witty, interesting look for my rooms," she says of her little downtown apartment. "I had my decorator cover the walls with bone-white huckaback. I had Muller's pick me out fifteen yards of books on assorted subjects. And I purchased a bottle of gin, a bottle of vermouth and a jar of cocktail onions, so that when I had acquired some friends I should be able to invite them up, to drink gibsons and admire my view of the Hudson River."

Poppy ends up marrying a cad — because what else? She gets by without a gun and without too much deception, except of the self-directed kind. Not without a few gibsons, though, because that would be a real crime.

CANADA DAY TIPPLES

They say the only truly Canadian cocktail is the Caesar, and that's fine as far as it goes. Which isn't very far. Sure, it's a tasty drink when mixed well (spicy, rim salt, heavy on the vodka), tossed back along with a zippy football pregame show or well-curled Brier final. We serve and drink them by the gallon around here, consuming more Mott's Clamato juice than anywhere else on earth. But the Bloody Mary with a squirt of clam juice goes back decades in New York mixology, damaging any claims to local provenance. We've made it ours, maybe, but we didn't invent it.

How better to celebrate Canada Day than by mixing a cold shaker of something a little more Canuck, even if you're the kind of Canadian who thinks non-beer drinking starts with rye-and-coke and stops at seven-and-seven. Most of these drinks have Canadian whisky in them, so be not afraid; just buy a big bottle of C.C. or Seagram's and start mixing.

First and best is a cocktail known simply as the Canadian. This is really a swish manhattan variation, using Triple Sec's rich citrus sweetness in place of the red vermouth. But just a couple of teaspoons of that, please, added to two good jiggers of whisky, with a dash of Angostura bitters and a half tea-spoon of bar sugar, for balance. Shake vigorously with cracked ice, and strain into a chilled cocktail glass. He shoots, he scores! *The Savoy Cocktail Book* has a 1930s variation that uses gum syrup instead of the sugar and Triple Sec, but that is too plain. Also ignore its bizarre alternative "Canadian" cocktail, a mix-ture of curaçao, sugar, lemon juice, and rum. Rum? Curaçao? Any Canadians drinking that are *lost*. Get the setting sun on your left-hand side and start walking.

Up to *la belle province*, which inspired the Quebec cocktail and its cousins the Habitant and the Trois Rivières. The basic Quebec calls for six parts whisky to two parts Amer Picon and two parts dry vermouth. Toss in one part maraschino liqueur and shake it all together with cracked ice. Strain and serve in a chilled cocktail glass. This drink also has manhattan over-tones, coming close to the so-called Perfect Manhattan, which splits dry and sweet vermouth half and half. A bit fussy to make, but once you get the hang of it you'll want to say, over and over, *my Canada includes the Quebec*. The Habitant uses a little less whisky than the Quebec, then adds fresh lemon juice and – yes, it's true – maple syrup; about a teaspoon each should do it. Again, shake it up well with cracked ice and serve in a chilled cocktail glass. You can add an orange-and-cherry "flag" garnish to this drink, but it's hard to imagine any *habitant*, even one willing to use a cocktail glass, putting up with that.

The Trois Rivières is more complicated still, a fair bit of intoxicating trouble, as fractious Quebeckers can be. Think of it as a francophile version of the Canadian, worth the hassle if you're in a federalist mood. Two big measures of whisky again, only this time add a half ounce of Dubonnet rouge and a tablespoon of Cointreau. Shake with ice, strain, and serve with a twist of orange. *Magnifique!*

Out on the Prairies grows the Canadian Daisy, a tall afternoon cooler that combines a teaspoon of raspberry syrup and some fresh lemon juice with two big shots of whisky. This is stirred with ice cubes, then poured into a chilled highball or collins glass and topped up with sparkling water. Float some brandy on the top and garnish with a few raspberries. For a truly Canadian touch, sub in saskatoons.

Things are a little less sparkly up in the Rockies, where the namesake of the Banff Cocktail can be found, a site for television festivals, artist retreats, and dewy youngsters with more looks than brains. Four parts whisky, one part Grand Marnier, one part kirschwasser. Add a dash of Angostura bitters, shake vigorously with cracked ice, strain, and serve in a chilled cocktail glass. Drink this too fast, especially at Banff altitude, and you'll be celebrating C-Day staring at the sky.

John A. Macdonald drank straight gin in place of water in the Commons, apparently, and ever since, gin has had a central place in Canadian drinking. So, for the Loyal Toast and beyond, try the Queen Elizabeth cocktail. That's six parts gin, one part dry vermouth, two teaspoons of Benedictine. Stir with ice, strain, and serve. Basically a dry gin martini with some aromatic herbal bite from those clever Catholic monks; the Counter-Reformation in a glass.

Or, finally, venture into the Hudson Bay: four parts gin, two parts cherry brandy, one part fresh orange juice, and a tablespoon of fresh lime. Oh, and throw in a glug of 151-proof rum while you're at it. Shake hard with ice and strain into a cold cocktail glass. Henry Hudson would approve: lime and orange to ward off scurvy, brandy and rum to generate inner warmth. No Northwest Passage, maybe, but two of those and you won't care.

CHAMPAGNE COCKTAIL

"Very few people now can afford unlimited champagne, and even if they could such extravagance would be most harmful and unpatriotic, just the very sort of thing that breeds socialism in the country."

Well, Gloria, Lady Bobbin – for it is she, nemesis of the Nancy Mitford novel *Christmas Pudding* (1932) – had one thing right. Very few people can afford the crates of Veuve or Moet their restless hearts desire. And that is too bad – though whether this is, in fact, the first recorded instance of the concept "champagne socialist" is a matter for scholars. A visitor to Compton Bobbin, the country estate where terrifying Lady

B is iron ruler and foul-mouthed local master of foxhounds, offers a solution.

"Why not have champagne cocktails instead?" he says, helpfully but tactlessly. "They are very economical, because you need only buy the cheapest sort of champagne, to which you add a little brandy and sugar, and people do seem to like them most awfully."

"No, Mr. Fisher, no cocktails in this house, thank you. I regard the cocktail habit as a most pernicious and disgusting one. Besides, people get rowdy enough on champagne alone, without adding brandy to it. Why, last year, at Lady Jenkins' party, the most disgraceful things happened. I actually saw that awful Hood boy, at supper, cramming a sausage down his ear, for a bet, I suppose."

Lady Bobbin's sense of patriotism carries the day, of course. When the proposed dance goes forward, she "remained true to her resolution that in *her* house there should be no champagne during the national crisis, and on every hand could soon be heard the groans and curses with which British youth greets the absence of any alcohol more fortifying than beer at its parties." Intimates of the dashing young scion of the family, an Eton schoolboy called Bobby with a predilection for gambling and dry gin, are invited to a cocktail bar upstairs, accentuating "the wretched sobriety of the other guests."

Which is all to say that, regardless of the dangers of socialism or aural sausage ingestion, you cannot regard the cocktail habit in quite the same pernicious light as Lady Bobbin, nor the addition of brandy as anything but, in general, a very good thing. Paul, the young mixologist coming to the rescue of the doomed dance, is on the money: a sparkly, hard-hitting champagne cocktail, by no means the effete chick drink it may appear, is just the thing to set a dreary party going. Even the most cracking bore can be made tolerable, if not interesting, by a couple of them; and they share the Dorothy Parker Martini Effect, in that three will find you under the table, four under the host.

As so often with the bubbles, however, a tricky drink. Not everyone likes a champagne cocktail, for one thing, but endeavour to persuade them that the time is right. "It's odd how one drinks different things in different places," muses Charlie Mortdecai, the disreputable art dealer and part-time crook from Kyril Bonfiglioli's aforementioned incomparable novels. "For instance, although I hate champagne cocktails, I always accept a couple from one particular mistress because a champagne cocktail, as anyone will tell you, gets to you where you live very fast and two such drinks enable me to ignore the grotesque schnozzle with which this particular lady has been endowed and to concentrate upon her other charms, which are of great distinction." Mortdecai's list of apposite place/drink pairings also includes a pub on Jersey where he invariably drinks a large scotch whisky with fresh orange juice, an Italian place in Oxford where brandy and soda is the norm, and Jules's bar in Jermyn Street for a standing order of Canadian whisky with ginger ale. All drinkers should have such mental maps.

So, anyway, inform any objectors that the cocktail will have the happy effect of making everyone more attractive to everyone else. But Paul's recipe is a bit off, for another thing. Don't just dump sugar and brandy into third-rate champers and hope for the best. Choose a decent sparkler in the double-sawbuck range, say a Domaine de Martinolles or a Cuvée Napa – neither of them from Champagne proper and so immune from the inflation that afflicts the genuine marques – and put it on ice. You might risk a Spanish cava or Prosecco, but be sure that it is very dry, almost bland, so as to offer a good platform for the brandy.

You'll want a good slug of that, about an ounce and a half, poured over a sugar cube that has been soaked in Angostura bitters at the bottom of a champagne flute. The brandy can be pretty much anything past the cooking-only neighbour-hood. No need for Hine or Martell VSOP, in other words, but stay away from those plastic bottles on the bottom shelf. Top up with the chilled wine, stir gently, and serve. Twist optional.

The recipe is simple but has to be strictly observed. The champagne cocktail must be elegance itself, the drink Cary Grant suggests he and Deborah Kerr down before dinner on board that ship in *An Affair to Remember* (1957) – though in fact they end up drinking pink champagne instead. But it's also a drink that can be both expensive and tacky if, for example, the barman has been told to use Courvoisier topped by Cristal: the Bling-Bling Special. Ritchie Cunningham and Potsy, contemplating a visit to Chicago in an old episode of *Happy Days*, worry that they'll be set on by B-girls who'll order champagne cocktails and bankrupt them in one round.

For a nice variation, replace cognac with calvados, the smart apple-tinged brandy from Normandy. Call it the Cavalier Cocktail. Or you can leave out the brandy altogether, as they do at the Rainbow Room in New York, but what's the thinking there?

You can even, if you're robust, go the other way and add more brandy. "How do you like your brandy, sir?" crippled old General Sternwood asks Philip Marlowe in *The Big Sleep* (1939), contemplating his mad daughter, his bad daughter, his lost friend, and blackmail. "I used to like mine with champagne," the general muses. "The champagne as cold as Valley Forge and about a third of a glass of brandy beneath it."

Try that and pretty soon you'll be sleeping the big sleep, all right. But it'll be cool sweet going.

HARVEY WALLBANGER WITH SIDECAR

O kay, it's really just a screwdriver with a slight variation, but to stop there undersells the Harvey Wallbanger's appeal, which is more cultural than mixological. Next time you're at the bar, scanning the array of bottles, thinking idle thoughts, look for the long thin one filled with – well, with piss-yellow fluid is the truth, the bottle itself reminiscent of a Florentine *carabinieri*'s firearm. This is Galliano, the banana-flavoured Franco-Italian liqueur that transforms a run-of-the-mill screwdriver, thoughtless choice of sorority sisters and Harvard squares, into the Wallbanger, preferred tipple of throwback swingers.

The Harvey Wallbanger glows with an aura of zany air-force circuit parties and madcap *Breakfast at Tiffany's* bashes where guys in dark suits and white shirts, with horn-rimmed glasses and grey hair, call everybody "baby" or "sweetheart" and plot to get lucky later. It is easy to mix, good to drink, and, most of all, fun to order. Sound out its goofy trochee/dactyl combo: HAR-vee WALL-bang-er. This is a drink way overdue for a comeback. The makers of Galliano, toiling away loyally since 1896 with few other venues to count on, will thank you.

So take a chilled collins glass and slosh in two big measures of vodka over some ice cubes. This book holds no views on the relative merits of vodka, all of them suspect products of root vegetables and dim northern climes, but Belvedere or Stolichnaya will do. Add orange juice, fresh squeezed if possible and Tropicana pulp if not. Unless it's for brunch the morning after getting lucky, go easy on the O.J. You want a drink, not a cooler. To finish, float a pony of Galliano on top. Now shoot your cuffs, straighten your narrow tie, and work the crowd, sweetheart.

But what is she drinking, your winsome prey, in her sleeveless Givenchy LBD, her hand-me-down pearls, and her Seven Sisters smile? She's not drinking anything until you fetch it, dope, so hop to it. You might be thinking champagne, or some cocktail variant thereof. But you would be wrong. Here's the news: this time, make hers a sidecar.

Nobody seems to know what the sidecar has to do with sidecars, though obviously anyone drinking them belongs there rather than behind the handlebars. Outside of esoteric motor sports or *Batman* comics, who even has occasion to see one? The liquid version is nevertheless the perfect bolt-on for your Wallbanging. While you're getting your vitamin C and potassium, she's getting quietly hammered. Vroom!

This is a drink with enviable lineage. In Nancy Mitford's loose-limbed Jazz Age comedy *Highland Fling* (1931), the sidecar is the cocktail penniless young aristocrats order to celebrate a rash engagement. Along with black coffee, it is Auntie Mame's breakfast of choice in the unimprovable 1958 Rosalind Russell film. In a *New Yorker* short story of a few years back, an old-school Manhattan father celebrates the engagement of his teenage daughter to her decade-older English teacher with sidecars all round. "We're a Sidecar family," booms the back-slapping old man. Now that's a toast.

Or consider this scene from a 1953 pulp novel, provenance uncertain but discovered not long ago in a Connecticut garage sale, called *Girl-Crazy Professor*, author one Florence Stonebraker (possibly not her real name). Helen Winters is a nineteen-year-old coed with flowing blonde hair, the curves of Rita Hayworth, and no compunction; Kevin Barbour is her easily tempted thirty-seven-year-old psychology professor; they are alone in his house. "After she had had three sidecars, Helen declared that she felt absolutely wonderful. She took off the satin sandals and danced around the room. She put them back on, perched herself on Kevin's desk, told him to give her a smoke and another drink. Then she crossed one leg high over the other and started to sing a song the cowboys had taught her. She made her voice low and husky, cocking her head to one side . . ." Another drink, you say? Absolutely.

(Not to worry: it ends well, with Helen getting non-fatally shot by a jealous ex-boyfriend and Kevin crashing his car, suffering concussion and pneumonia, but eventually going back to his hot twenty-nine-year-old wife, who basically blames herself for all his philandering. 1953! Was Florence Stonebraker possibly, maybe, just perhaps, not a woman?)

"The usual Side Car has equal parts of the three ingredients," says *The ABC of Cocktails*, a slim, indispensable volume also from 1953. The ingredients in question, all shaken hard with cracked ice and strained into a cocktail glass, are brandy, lemon juice, and Triple Sec. For a more up-to-date version, ease up on the Triple Sec and lemon, and add more brandy. The ABCers themselves suggest six parts brandy, two parts lemon juice, and one part Triple Sec. *The New York Bartender's Guide*, meanwhile, calls for four, two, two, a scheme agreed to by *The Savoy Cocktail Book*, though the latter specifies Cointreau in place of Triple Sec, a distinction without a difference.

Be warned that some modern bartenders will offer you a weaker number, with lemon mix, one shot of brandy, and just a dash of Cointreau. This is the pale cousin sidecar, anemic next to the genuine robust article: call it the Training Wheel. More brandy, please, more Triple Sec, real lemons. And shake hard for that nice top-of-the-glass froth.

The resulting drink is not only pretty, an aromatic amber cloud, but sharply satisfying; it puts in the shade all those modern chick drinks, the fruity cosmopolitans and metropolitans everywhere swilled by the trying-too-hard *Sex and the City* crowd. Oranges and lemons compete with the brandy's distilled grapes for a dose of sweet and sour perfection, lighter tasting than you might expect from a brandy-based concoction. The brandy, as always, should be good but need not be special, let alone very special old pale; don't waste your money on pricey cognac. Use plain Marquis de Villard or, if you're feeling dirty-old-man cheeky, try the recent label from upstate New York called, of all things, Christian Brothers.

Now banish all thoughts of age, compatibility, and the reckless immaturity of most humans under forty, especially the good-looking ones. She's drinking, you're drinking. What a swell party it is, baby!

THE GAME

Censorious people might say that caring about a football game between two barely competent gangs of brainiac college students is evidence of a defect of character. But don't try telling this to anyone in New Haven or Cambridge, especially around the end of November, when the annual Harvard-Yale football match, known as "The Game," galvanizes crimson and blue armies.

Sure, three things: (1) Penn or Dartmouth has usually locked up the league title already, (2) this isn't Pac-10 football at the best of times, and (3) it can be pretty effing cold. On the other hand, three other things: (1) the bands offer classic fight songs like "Louie Louie" and "White Punks on Dope," (2) you might be sitting next to Benno Schmidt, the former president of Yale who had a cameo in a Woody Allen movie, and (3) there's always the chance to see some raccoon-coated old dude, glass in hand, dissolving into tears when the wishbone formation once again fails to generate a first down.

The best part of The Game is not inside the stadium, however. Yale-Harvard tail-gating is, predictably, less barbecue-and-beer next to the F-150 than champagne-and-caviar alongside the Range Rover. Crystal and silver are so common a sight that, on a sunny day, the combined sparkle spins a web of blinding refraction. Out here you can enjoy another little Harvard-Yale contest, over The Drink.

The Harvard and Yale namesake cocktails are superb old-time mixes invented in New York at the respective clubs operating there for graduates of the two colleges. Some people think all things Ivy are indistinguishable, others that you can tell a Yalie a mile off (he's the Wall Street m-and-a jerk in red suspenders); but whatever the truth there, the drinks couldn't be more different. Choosing between them says something about what school of thought, if not what school, you attend.

The Yale is simpler, a martini variation. Add a small splash of maraschino liqueur and three dashes of orange bitters to a standard four-to-one gin and dry vermouth base. Shake hard with cracked ice and pour into a chilled cocktail glass, with a little curl of lemon peel as garnish. The resulting cool pinkish drink, not the Drano blue we might expect from Elihu Yale's venerable school, is well balanced, tasty, and elegant.

If the Yale has class, the Harvard has power. Mix four parts brandy with one part sweet vermouth, adding a big splash of fresh lemon juice, a splash of grenadine, and a dash of Angostura bitters. Shake it all with cracked ice, strain, and serve up. The Harvard bears some similarity to the sidecar (brandy, lemon juice, and Triple Sec) and is a well-heeled cousin of the metropolitan (brandy, sweet vermouth, and bitters). The lemon juice and grenadine make it more trouble than either but also richer and more interesting. College boy comes to the city.

Which of them wins out is a matter of taste, not touch-downs. But if you can't decide, or if you attended some place with an even worse football team, there's always the Princeton. That's six parts gin, two parts ruby port, and three to five dashes Angostura bitters. Shake, strain, and serve up in a chilled cocktail glass, with a lemon twist for garnish. Not many people would think of mixing gin and port, let alone in the same glass, but that's why Princeton houses the Institute for Advanced Study.

Finally, if all this football and college-boy stuff gets you down, if pigskin and gridiron fail to inspire, if for you fall means the twilight of the boys of summer – if, in short, you are a baseball person – take a trip, like the down-and-out sportswriter of Richard Ford's 1986 novel, to Cooperstown,

New York. There's summer-stock opera, memorabilia galore, Doubleday Field, and the Hall of Fame. There's also, when it's warm, the wide verandah of the Otesaga Hotel, looking out over Lake Otsego, James Fenimore Cooper's famous "Glimmerglass." Unfold yourself into an aged Adirondack chair, scoop some peanuts, and order a Cooperstown. Tell the barman four parts gin, plus one part dry vermouth and one part sweet. Shake, strain, and serve cold with a sprig of fresh mint as garnish.

And now, if you're lucky, maybe Hank Aaron will stroll by, and you can raise a hand and say, between sips, "Howdy, Hammer!" and he will smile vaguely and say nothing. Maybe you're bothering him, but that's okay, because the next sip, and that moment, perfectly squeezed into the gap, make your day complete – a personal home run.

WAUGH FOR WINTER

"I like this bad set and I like getting drunk at luncheon," Charles Ryder tells his uptight cousin Jasper in Evelyn Waugh's *Brideshead Revisited* (1945), and who can blame him? Few luxuries surpass writing off a day before it is half over. *Brideshead* is booze-braised fiction, a sweet pear poached in brandy. Champagne and whisky flow all too freely. But sunny days of strawberries and Château Peyraguey, warm summer evenings of wine-tasting that prompt doomed Sebastian Flyte to ask, "Ought we to be drunk *every* night?" ("Yes, I think so," Charles says), soon turn cold and dark. Sebastian, the enchanting young Catholic aristo, descends into hopeless, alcoholic wretchedness.

Even in his comic novels, Waugh writes with a wintry heart. He is like champagne itself: bubbly happiness with a brutal morning, or sometimes afternoon, after.

Decline and Fall (1928), the Jazz Age revival of Voltaire's *Candide*, describes how impoverished schoolmaster Paul Pennyfeather meets his complicated fate. Discovered by society hostess Margot Beste-Chetwynde, then engaged to her, Paul begins drinking at 10 a.m. on his wedding day and then, right after his second luncheon brandy, is arrested for white-slaving and put in prison – where, later, his death will be faked so he can return to a quiet life of theological ministry. His fellow former schoolmaster, the doubting clergyman called Prendergast, gets drunk at a school sports day and fires the starting pistol into the foot of Little Lord Tangent, son of Lady Circumference, who later loses the leg, then dies from blood poisoning; Prendergast himself, restored to holy orders, becomes the chaplain of the prison where Paul is sent – where he is beheaded by a psychotic inmate. Agatha Runcible of *Vile Bodies* (1930) has whisky for breakfast followed by a bottle of champagne and, feeling "buoyant and detached (as one should if one drinks a great deal before luncheon)," enters a car race, crashes, gets hospitalized, goes mad, and later expires in an aside.

As a satirist, Waugh liked, in the words of Robert Towne, to "leave a lot of hats on the ground." No happy endings, just endings – a world of glitter and emptiness, of vice without punishment and sin without redemption. Consequently, he depicts drink from a position of vast fear and inside knowledge, just one of his manifold literary virtues. There are only a few cocktails to be found in his work, and that is a shame. (His friend Nancy Mitford was more that way inclined.) But as the nights close in, those few cocktails to be found in Waugh's corpus offer some worthwhile winter options, cold drinks for cold weather.

First, an acquired taste from early in *Brideshead*. Anthony Blanche, the strutting, stuttering Oxford aesthete with his eyes on Charles and Sebastian both, invites Charles out for dinner. He wants to poison the youngster against his beautiful friend: "Of course, those that have charm don't really need brains. . . . Tell me candidly, have you ever heard Sebastian say *anything* you have remembered for five minutes?" They end their meal with "Real G-g-green Chartreuse, made before the expulsion of the monks" but begin it with a cocktail, or four. Charles reports: "At the George bar he ordered 'Four Alexander cocktails, please,' ranged them before him with a loud 'Yum-yum' which drew every eye, outraged, upon him. . . . 'One, two, three, four, down the red lane they go. *How* the students stare!'"

That's two parts gin, two parts crème de cacao, and two parts light cream, all shaken with cracked ice and strained into a cocktail class, served with a sprinkle of ground nutmeg on top. As Blanche says, "a delicious concoction" but on the sickly side: "the sweet and creamy cocktail had tainted his breath," Charles recalls, leaning away. The Brandy Alexander, better known since its 1970s fern-bar revival, naturally uses brandy in place of gin; Alexander's Sister, meanwhile, has an extra half ounce of gin and crème de menthe, white or green as you like, in place of the cacao.

More manly is Black Velvet, the favoured cocktail of bright young things about to be obliterated by war in *Put Out More Flags* (1942). Alastair Digby-Vane-Trumpington "opened bottles and began mixing stout and champagne in a deep jug. . . . They had always drunk this sour and invigorating draught," known familiarly, per upper-class slang, as "Blackers" and, here, for preference drunk before noon in the suite of a society lady who likes to receive visitors while bathing. For a single serving, try a quarter pint each of cold champagne and stout or porter, poured slowly (not mixed) into a chilled highball glass.

If any of that seems dreary, just remember that the season can also see bleak change into joyous. In the same novel, gorgeous Angela Lyne loses her grip on things one winter in a service flat "as smart and non-committal as herself." "Angela never drank cocktails except in private," the narrator says. "There was something about them which bore, so faintly as to be discernible to no one but herself, a suggestion of good fellowship and good cheer; an infinitely small invitation to familiarity, derived perhaps from the days of prohibition when gin had ceased to be Hogarthian and had become chic."

So no gin, and no company, for lovely Angela; but that doesn't mean no drinking. "And so Angela, who hated human contact on any but her own terms, never drank cocktails except in solitude. Lately all her days seemed to be spent alone. . . . She mixed herself a large cocktail; the principal ingredients were vodka and Calvados." The line echoes one found in *Decline and Fall*. Paul Pennyfeather's young pupil Peter Beste-Chetwynde, whose mother Paul is to marry, is an enthusiastic aficionado of mixology even at the tender age of sixteen. "He makes them rather well," his proud mother says. Indeed he does. Welcoming a guest to their country house, "Peter mixed him a formidable cocktail, the principal ingredients of which were absinthe and vodka." Mrs. Beste-Chetwynde, later to be Margot Metroland, favours something described in the novel as an "absinthe frappé," and perhaps best left to the imagination.

Calvados sounds a rather more palatable companion for vodka, however. Waugh doesn't name Angela's ultrasmart drink, but let us follow the example of hockey-loving, Tums-chewing bartender Joe Bell in Truman Capote's novella *Breakfast at Tiffany's*. Talking to the story's narrator about their mutual friend Holly Golightly, Joe says, "Let me build you a drink. Something new. They call it a White Angel." That's half vodka and half gin, no vermouth at all, all shaken and strained into a cocktail glass. Call Angela's even better drink the Winter Angel, then, and try it this way: six parts vodka to two parts calvados, shake hard with cracked ice, strain into a chilled cocktail glass. Garnish with a lime twist. The distilled apple of calvados will make the vodka sing a frosty seraphic descant. Angela eventually emerges from her funk, and we trust she realized then that this is too good a cocktail to drink alone. You don't have to wait: call a warm friend now.

PAPA CUBA

Hemingway didn't like cigars, apparently, either because the scent of tobacco, lit or not, could be picked up by the big-game animals he liked to stalk; or because smoking impaired his sense of smell while stalking them; or maybe because he was just, underneath it all, doomed. A cigar-smoking man takes a philosophical view of the world; or else, like Rex Mottram in *Brideshead Revisited*, he uses them as a sort of thrice-daily prop to add gravitas to political ambition, being after all just your average ruthless Canadian buccaneering among snooty Brits between the world wars. That's a different kind of anchor than what Salinger's Zooey needs: "The cigars are ballast, sweetheart. Sheer ballast. If he didn't have a cigar to hold on to, his feet would leave the ground. We'd never see our Zooey again."

Readers will recall that it is this piece of verbal stunt flying that makes Franny realize it is Zooey, not her brother Buddy, on the other end of the phone-line. Zooey, imitating Buddy, is talking about Zooey in order to get Franny to stop copying Buddy. It's all very Salinger. Anyway, the point is that the well-balanced cigar-smoking man drinks to enjoy life, not to dull the screams of his inner demons. Poor Papa. Could a timely smoke have saved him?

For those who have a taste for both vices, there are two classes of cigar-friendly cocktails, the choice a matter of latitude. If you find yourself in the chilly northern quadrant, you'll want a warming amber distillate: whisky, Canadian or scotch as fancy dictates, or even brandy. Fire up your chocolatey Monte Cristo No. 4 with a smooth Perfect Manhattan or, better still, a fireside Rusty Nail. That's four parts blended scotch and two parts Drambuie, over ice, in a chilled old-fashioned glass. There's a variation we like to call the Rusty Claymore, with the underused scotch liqueur Glayva taking the place of Drambuie – a celtophile's nuance.

If you want even more spreading warmth in your frozen post-shinny limbs, go the brandy route, either solo or with a friendly mix. A splash of soda from the library spritzer makes for the traditional English bracer that might be known as the Peter Wimsey Special, after Dorothy Sayers's pukka amateur detective; or, mixed with more brandy and less bubbly, the Bertie Wooster Whoosher, as ordered here in a signature exchange from Wodehouse's *The Inimitable Jeeves* (1924):

> "I say, Jeeves," I said.
> "Sir."
> "Mix me a stiffish brandy and soda."
> "Yes, sir."
> "Stiffish, Jeeves. Not too much soda, but splash the brandy about a bit."
> "Very good, sir."

Very good is right, especially if the brandy is Napoleon or Hine. Instead of soda you might try adding a dollop of Benedictine, those clever monks at work again. The B-and-S is good just by itself, but the B&B is best taken over ice in an old-fashioned glass. You can buy B&B premixed, of course, but try stirring yourself to get an optimum blend, and have a spice-nosed Cohiba Corona Especiale at the ready. That will restore the tissues eftsoons and right speedily, as Bertie might put it.

Down south, in Papa and Che country, where they actually make the things, you can break away from the leather armchair to enjoy yourself more robustly with deep-sea fishing or permanent revolution. Cool Havana breezes, the ones that enabled Hem "to work as well there . . . [as] anywhere in the world," will waft away the swirling blue crescents from your Fonseca Delicias or Romeo y Julieta No. 3. These lighter smokes go better with rum, and fortunately for you, there's lots of it about.

Try a Cuba Libre, the old standby, rum and coke enlivened by fresh lime juice. Go heavy on the rum, Bacardi White Label for preference, and pour into a chilled and ice-filled collins glass. Or bust out a mojito, lately revived by New York fashion but not to be avoided for all that. Sip the cool rum and mint flavours while blowing circles in the air from a velvety La Gloria Cubana Sobroso. The common mojito is actually a crystal variation, with rum, lime juice, sugar, and mint, all served over ice with soda. Try it straight up instead: four parts light rum, two parts fresh lime juice, a teaspoon of bar sugar, five or six bruised mint leaves, and a dash of Angostura bitters. Shake with cracked ice and strain into a chilled cocktail glass.

Finally, in tribute to Papa himself, there's the Papa Doble, a drink he made famous at Havana's El Floridita bar, adding it to the long list of joints that witnessed scenes of Hemingway drunkenness: Harry's in Venice, the Ritz in Paris, Sloppy Joe's in Key West, Chicote's in Madrid.

It's a daiquiri, of course, a drink largely annexed by umbrella-and-cherry slurpees with strawberries and peaches, like gelato through a straw. But don't be fooled. The real daiquiri is just big slugs of rum with fresh citrus juice. The Papa Doble, Hem's preferred double-daq, is anybody's idea of a manly tipple: eight parts Bacardi White Label, the juice of two limes and half a grapefruit, two dashes of maraschino liqueur. Mix with shaved ice and serve in a chilled collins glass. El Floridita legend has it that Hemingway drank sixteen of them in one sitting, a formidable ingestion of vitamin C if nothing else. Nothing else like sixty-plus ounces of rum.

You could flame up a big stogie with that drink, a Hoyo de Monterrey Double Corona or maybe a Partagas Churchill – one of those dirigible-sized honkers named after the corpulent British prime minister, allegedly invented in response to medical advice that he limit himself to one cigar a day. But a man has to smoke a cigar that fits his face, so you might prefer a Partagas Serie D or a Monte No. 3 instead. More heft than your usual, but not stupidly so.

"I like a cigar to really draw," Count Mippipopolous says in Hemingway's *The Sun Also Rises* (1926), making a ceremony of wielding his gold cutter. Typically, he captures in seven words a sentiment that occupies Hans Castorp, in Thomas Mann's *The Magic Mountain* (1924), for ten pages. Either way, the point is taken: a good cigar *lets you smoke it*, being neither a test of lung power nor a suck on a hollow tube. Cut, light, draw.

And scent or no scent, have at your elbow a worthy mix to make its acquaintance. Here's to your good mental health, and *viva la revolución*.

BOSTON COCKTAILS

Time, they say, begins on Opening Day. Well, actually it was Thomas Boswell who said it, in his 1984 book of the same name, but now everybody does, and why not? Especially in the slushy cold-weather towns of the Northeast, where baseball maintains such an unlikely hold on otherwise pure hockey or football country, the promise of the spring thaw quickens the pulse of diehard fans with Diehard batteries. Come April, chilled baseball souls everywhere grind and turn over.

Sometimes, quirk of the calendar, one sacred observance of fair and foul rebirth aligns with another, and Opening Day actually falls on Good Friday. It didn't happen this year, alas,

Easter coming early, but think of it: there's a conjunction of yearning and hope and resurrection, the stuff of gospel hymns and Kris Kristofferson songs. Say it with us, sing it out, sing it loud: Jesus Died on Opening Day!

On the third day he rose from the dead, and in the eighty-sixth summer the Red Sox, too, walked again. They also stole, homered, and ran, all the way to the big title. Generations of Sox fans went to their graves without witnessing it, but there it was, implausible but right, down three games to none against the Bronx-based Wal-Mart of baseball, clawing hairily back, neanderthals of resistance, upsetting Steinbrenner's Stormtroopers, those clean-jawed, neck-trimmed millionaire-automatons, on the way to an easy Series. Idiots everywhere, to use Johnny Damon's sobriquet, rejoiced.

But not for long. Bostonians, unused to victory, scanned the horizon for a cloud amid all the silver lining, and found it. Callow moneyball GM Theo Epstein, they said, had blown his budget and skill on a one-time title! He'd left the franchise high and dry. One ace was hobbled and bleeding from the ankle, another had absconded to the New York Mets, and the third was a goateed knuckleballer, for crying out loud. Damon moved to the hated Yankees and cut his hair. The rest was a posse of semi-talented, bedhead misfits past their sell-by dates. Rejoice again! There's still something to complain about!

The Red Sox did not repeat in 2005, and they might not even compete for another eight decades; but let's pause every year anyway, on the cusp of a new 182-game lifespan, and give some due to the best self-convinced underdogs baseball has ever seen. "They lie low," the columnist Norman Chad wrote, "lull you into a false sense of security, then just when you are most relaxed – bang! – it's the woe-is-me-and-the-curse-of-the-Bambino-and-don't-get-me-started-on-Bill-Buckner-and-sure-now-we've-got-our-first-World-Series-title-since-1918-but-we're-still-20-championships-behind-the-Bronx-Bombers routine. It takes a nickel to get a Red Sox fan started and maybe 50 bucks to shut him up." Four Beantown cocktails, then, equal to a series sweep, in salute to the rude old racist city, with its ups and downs and toxic inferiority complex – something Canadians can relate to.

First and best, the plain Boston Cocktail. That's three parts gin to two parts apricot brandy, enlivened with a teaspoon each of fresh lemon juice and grenadine. Sluice it all into a shaker with a handful of cracked ice and give it a rattling ride, like the T out to Fenway. Strain into a chilled cocktail glass, no garnish. Fruity and sharp, not too sweet, but with a rocket-fuel pop like Curt Schilling's old fastball.

There's a Boston Sour, so called because it varies the standard whisky sour with some Beacon Hill nicety, not least in the form of an egg white. Mix it with four parts Canadian whisky, plus two parts fresh lemon juice and a teaspoon of bar sugar. Shake vigorously with cracked ice to get a good old froth, then strain into a chilled sour glass. Garnish with a lemon-and-maraschino flag. A bit prissy, maybe, but with a solid whisky bottom.

Now a couple of rum-based drinks, hearkening romantically back to the pre-1812 days, when Boston was far above New York's Dutch obscurity and Philadelphia's neo-classical grace, not just the cradle of revolution but a cosmopolitan port. Barkys and sloops and schooners from all over the planet brought spices, danger, and drink.

So: The Boston Cooler mixes four parts light rum with one part fresh lemon juice and a half teaspoon of bar sugar. Shake with ice, strain into a chilled highball glass over ice cubes, and top up with sparkling water. Stir and garnish with a lemon twist. Great for a midsummer day game.

And finally, favourite of Back Bay broads everywhere, the Boston Sidecar, an elegant rum touch-up to the basic item. The usual trio of brandy, Triple Sec, and lemon juice, here present at one part each, are joined by three parts light rum. Shake with cracked ice, strain, and serve in a chilled cocktail glass.

The rum-runners are long gone, and the ships in the harbour these days are mostly powered by oil, not wind, but that's a nice mouthful of East Coast history. If you can, order one in the dim leathery glory of the Oak Bar at the Copley Plaza Hotel, where cocktails come in little glass carafes with their own ice buckets, enough for two drinks.

Take a sip and ask the bartender if there's enough starting pitching. There isn't, because there never is; but ask anyway.

ANGLER'S and JACK ROSE

People always remember the bull-fighting scenes in Hemingway's *The Sun Also Rises*, but those of us with a less bloodthirsty disposition know the book is really about fly fishing. Yes, it's true. Right in the middle of that laconic, generation-defining tale of ruthless Lady Brett Ashley, "built with curves like the hull of a racing yacht," as Jake Barnes puts it, is a miniature masterpiece of angling literature.

The story is set in midsummer, high season for trout in the north of Spain. Also, Brett isn't there, which means irritating Princeton boxer Robert Cohn isn't either, or Brett's feckless fiancé, Michael, or her fancy young bullfighter beau. Just Jake and his pal Bill Gorton, some sort of journalism associate, and a goofy Englishman named Harris who ties his own flies. Jake and Bill hike into the country around Burguete, near Roncesvalles, and fall on the trout-filled Irati River, fast-flowing and cold. In one glorious day they land ten fat browns using double-tapered line and McGinty flies.

Actually, that's not quite true. Bill uses the fly and catches four, each of them bigger than the six Jake manages to land using worms. Worms practically constitute cheating – "You lazy bum!" Bill says – but we forgive him. They wrap the fish in cool leaves, eat some cold chicken, drink two bottles of red wine, nap, and then hike all the way back to their inn, long miles away, in time to watch the sunset. "Listen," Bill says to Jake as they share a last drink. "You're a hell of a good guy, and I'm fonder of you than anybody on earth. I couldn't tell you that in New York. It'd mean I was a faggot." The truth of male bonding, compactly expressed.

A prodigious amount of drinking gets done in the novel, its characters pretty much drunk all the time. Beer, wine, port, brandy, whisky, champagne, and Pernod are all consumed in quantity. (The last, Jake muses, "tastes like licorice and it has a good uplift, but it drops you just as far.") The only cocktails mentioned are the dry gin martini and the Jack Rose: one too common nowadays to need a recipe, the other mostly, alas, forgotten and deserving a revival.

Given the right occasion, Jake will take either. First, in a scene to curdle anyone's liver, Jake drinks three martinis before lunch at the Palace Hotel Bar in Madrid, telling the barman each time to add an olive, then he and Brett down four – count 'em, four – bottles of rioja over lunch.

"It's funny what a wonderful gentility you get in the bar of a big hotel," Jake tells her as they're drinking their martinis.

"Barmen and jockeys are the only people who are polite any more."

"No matter how vulgar a hotel is, the bar is always nice."

"It's odd."

"Bartenders have always been fine."

Sure they have. A few weeks earlier, Jake is waiting for Brett at the Hotel Crillon in Paris. Naturally she doesn't turn up, "so about quarter to six I went down to the bar and had a Jack Rose with George the barman." George would have known without looking that that's four parts applejack or Calvados, one part fresh lemon or lime juice, and a teaspoon of grenadine, all shaken with cracked ice and served in a chilled cocktail glass with a twist of lemon.

The genius of early Hemingway is the effortless float from city to country and back, from wine drunk on a riverbank to the polished glasses and smart white jackets of the urban bar. Case in point (another example of Papa's keen grasp of male bonding): together in Paris, before the implosion of their friendship over Brett, Jake and Cohn meet for a drink. Cohn looks at the various bottles in their bins around the wall, the staggered array of potables mirrored in the space behind the barman.

"This is a good place," he says.

"There's a lot of liquor," Jake agrees.

It's a shame Hemingway missed the cocktail that straddles both worlds, the simple grace of outdoor pursuits joined by some urban sophistication: the Angler's Cocktail.

This is a gin concoction, and a fine one too, cool, textured, and tasty. Take four parts gin, Tanqueray or Beefeater for preference, and mix with three dashes Angostura bitters, three dashes orange bitters, and three dashes grenadine. Shake briefly with some cracked ice, then strain into an old-fashioned glass with a couple of ice cubes. A bit like a pink gin, from the Angostura, but with a sweet little kick of fruit. You can sub in a tablespoon of Triple Sec or Cointreau for the orange bitters and get a stronger mix we like to call the Smooth Cast. Or, if you're in the mood for a long drink, mix the basic Angler's and then serve on the rocks, topped up with some tonic water: the Angler's Tonic.

During the first cold month of the trout season, all you'd want after a day on the water is a big slug of single-malt whisky. But for those glorious May and early June days, the ones that start cold and slowly warm, the trout rising smartly for their food – or a fly that looks just like it – the Angler's is an ideal mix. Back at the cabin, tired and happy, just thinking about dinner, a perfect sundowner for the man with a heavy creel and a light heart.

And tomorrow it rises again.

SUMMERTIME

I t's the Fourth of July in Eugene O'Neill's play *Ah, Wilderness!* (1933) and young Dick Miller, bookish, naive but full of extravagant longing and world-beating schemes, wants adventure beyond the bounds of the Sachem Club picnic or stiff family dinner. He busts out, and into the usual O'Neill pitfalls of drink, women, and bad company.

The latter comes in the form of Wint, a Yale College smoothie down to the shore on summer vacation. With his letterman sweater and slicked-back hair, Wint thinks he is, in a phrase favoured by Dick's smart-aleck kid sister, "the whole cheese." He wants company for an evening trip to the Pleasant Beach House, local "secret house of shame," where "swift babies" and "candy kiddoes" can be had for the price of a tipple or two. Count Dick in!

The drink is a sloe gin fizz, possibly the only cocktail (as with high-school girls of yore) that Dick knows. His new friend Belle, certainly swift, thinks Dick is too slow: she instructs the surly Beach House waiter to slosh some actual gin into Dick's glass. Call this new concoction the Sloe Dick Fizz, and mix it, advisedly, this way: four parts sloe gin, two parts gin, three parts fresh lemon juice, and a splash of syrup in a cocktail shaker, with cracked ice. Agitate, then strain into a chilled highball or collins glass over ice cubes. Fill with sparkling water and garnish with a lemon slice. Drink it fast, kiddo.

Sloe gin, a cordial distilled from overripe sloe plums, isn't everyone's poison, to be sure; it's sweet to the point of sickly. But a little can support a decent midsummer cooler, especially here with the extra gin to give the drink character as well as kick. There is a straight-up sloe gin cocktail, too, which is six parts of the stuff mixed with a teaspoon of dry vermouth and a couple of dashes of Angostura bitters, all shaken with ice, then strained into a chilled cocktail glass. You could dick with that one by halving the sloe gin and replacing with gin gin. Not bad at all.

What about Belle, meanwhile? Well, she's drinking gin rickeys, another breezy long drink for those hot July nights. That's four parts gin plus two parts fresh lime juice over ice, in a chilled highball glass, filled with sparkling water. Nothing drastic happens between Dick and Belle, by the way, and he returns to the family bosom and the arms of his true love, the swell unswift girl next door, in time for sunset.

Things are not so rosy for a different starry-eyed romantic, in another scene featuring gin rickeys, from another writer who knew his way around a bottle. Tom Buchanan serves them to Nick, Daisy, Jordan, and Gatsby during an ill-advised summer lunch on a hot, hot day on Long Island. "Gatsby took up his drink," Nick tells us. "'They certainly look cool,' he said, with visible tension."

"You look so cool," Daisy echoes to the pink-suited Gatsby, in her voice full of money. "You always look so cool." It's this breathless compliment that lets her husband, Tom, know that Daisy is in love with Gatsby – Gatsby with his movie-star parties and cocktail bars stocked with exotic cordials the young flapper girls have never heard of. Now brutish, uncool Tom rouses himself to open insult and the chain of roadside events that will encompass Gatsby's ruin.

You know the story. They drive into the city, this volatile group of friends and neighbours, then get a room at the Plaza, now with Tom's mistress and some other hapless misfits along for the ride. Tom has a quart bottle of bourbon wrapped in a towel; a waiter brings mint and crushed ice: mint juleps all round. But tempers flare, confessions are demanded, and the drinks never get made. In one of American literature's best-known non sequiturs, Nick realizes it's his birthday. Everyone leaves in a confusion of cars. "So we drove on," Nick says, "toward death through the cooling twilight."

A little heavy for your own twilight hour, so rewrite the ending of one American classic, at least for a moment, by mixing another. Mint julep is a down-home favourite at Derby season, of course, but it's not too shabby anytime, especially if you're a fan of bourbon, memorably labelled "the brownest of the brown liquors" by recurrent, alcoholic *Simpsons* lawyer Lionel Hutz. In a slightly more elevated, if *outré*, form, it is the favourite drink of an eccentric Miami art collector described in Harold Acton's louche 1965 novel *Old Lamps for New*, who loots the Lido for canvases "good, bad, and indifferent." These fill up a Palladian villa he's had built on the Florida coast, along with accessories worthy of Vegas: "the gondola he had imported to Miami with two gigantic gondoliers who waited on him at meals and sang O Sole Mio on the terrace while the sun went down." But no Prosecco for this wealthy wackjob: "The gondola served as a floating bar where he mixed his own mint juleps."

Here's how he did it. Combine fresh mint leaves and a tablespoon of simple syrup in a chilled highball glass. Muddle the mint with a spoon to release the flavour and aroma. Fill with shaved ice, then chase six parts of bourbon after it. Garnish with a sprig of mint. Don't get hung up on those Kentucky and Louisiana versus Tennessee niceties; it's too hot for arguing. Either Jim or Jack will do nicely. Sub in gin for the bourbon and it's called a gin smash, which is nice.

"You hit the spot, like a balmy breeze on a night in May," sang Anita O'Day, once upon a time. "You hit the spot, like a cool mint julep on a summer day." That voice hits the spot too, not full of money, maybe, but of summer's rich promise. "I had to fall, 'cause you got so much on the ball."

Now that's cool.

THE PONIES

Tipples are an essential accessory for the sporting set —
those people Hazlitt long ago called "the fancy," the ones
who follow the action, enter a book, take a flutter. While it
may be dangerous for punters to combine drink with wagering, that usually doesn't stop them. (They're gamblers, after
all.) Horse-racing and smart drinks thus have a long association, not least because there's always more time between races
than you can fill with consulting the form or floating trifecta
options. Whether drinking away your winnings or drowning
your losses, cocktails are there.

As noted, several of the many rival etymologies for the
word *cocktail* have a naggy canter. In the time of Henry VIII,

when that fine monarch was attempting to breed better steeds by crossing native British ponies with sleek Arabians, mixed-breed or quarter-horses routinely had their tails docked – a practice with us still. As a result, mixed things generally became known as cocktails. Rival linguists say "cocktail" was a common usage for high-spirited horses who raise their plumage during periods of intoxicated excitement. Neither camp (let's call them the dockers and the lifters) has much to say about the so-called cocktails of illegal substances now sometimes discovered in the bloodstream of winning long shots.

Anyway, happy are we who can sample a broad range of gee-gee-themed drinks, a neglected subgenre at the intersection of two noble traditions. The sly horse thieves in William Faulkner's *The Reivers* (1962) content themselves with homemade whisky – "half a jug of rotgut, mainly lye and red pepper," one grouses. That doubled complaint, that the whisky stinks and there's only half a jug of it, marks Faulkner as the origin of the old Catskills joke: "The food here is terrible," says one woman. "Yes," her friend replies, "and the portions are so small." (Woody Allen thought this a good metaphor for life generally.)

You can afford to back a wider field than rusty-still moonshine. Try a Belmont Stakes for starters. Triple Crown races are spring jewels, when freshness counts; their namesake drinks, by contrast, are good anytime. Combine four parts vodka, two parts gold rum, one part each strawberry liqueur and fresh lime juice, and a teaspoon of grenadine. Mix with cracked ice as if applying the whip down the stretch. Strain into a chilled cocktail glass and garnish with a twist of orange. Bright red, tart, and tasty.

Or how about a Preakness. Shake four parts blended whisky, two parts sweet vermouth, and a teaspoon of Benedictine with some ice, then strain into a chilled cocktail glass. Garnish with a lemon twist. That's pretty much a Rob Roy with Benedictine added, but the addition shows: pace yourself there, jockey boy.

There is a Kentucky Cocktail (bourbon and pineapple juice) and a Derby Special Cocktail (rum, Cointreau, and orange juice), but no Kentucky Derby Cocktail – the mint julep rules in Louisville, and we say fine. Just remember that, as P.G. Wodehouse warns, juleps are "insidious things. They creep up on you like a baby sister and slide their little hands into yours and the next thing you know the judge is telling you to pay the clerk of the court fifty dollars."

Ask for an Aqueduct Cocktail instead: four parts vodka, a splash each of apricot brandy, white curaçao, fresh lemon and fresh lime, all combined and shaken with ice. Strain into a chilled cocktail glass, garnish with a lemon twist. A well-balanced entry, this, solid and reliable, good legs. The Saratoga Cocktail, meanwhile, combines six parts brandy with a splash of lemon juice and one of maraschino liqueur, plus a big dollop of pineapple juice. Sidecar-ish in form, with a smart burst out of the gate and a strong finish.

The Jockey Club Cocktail is another old-school mix with a twist of new. Four parts gin are joined by one part fresh lemon juice, a half teaspoon of white crème de cacao, and a dash of Angostura bitters. Shake with cracked ice, strain, and serve in a chilled conical. That mix of flavours may sound a little odd but they come together nicely right around the clubhouse turn.

That little scrapper Seabiscuit is more famous now, thanks to the recent book and movie, but once upon a time a horse called Man O'War was even better known, the Bucephalus of the modern era. The Man O'War Cocktail is a big runner, too, with four parts bourbon, two parts each Triple Sec and fresh lime juice, and one part sweet vermouth. Mix with ice, shake, and strain into a cold cocktail glass. If you're used to drinking manhattans in Manhattan, where they use bourbon instead of the proper rye, this will taste familiar, only better, the orange and lime rounding things out with class. Scratch sweet vermouth for dry to get a less sugary result.

Finally, an old thoroughbred lately making a comeback. The Horse's Neck is a drink whose name is much disputed – gift horse? horse's mouth? – but whose qualities transcend argument. Fittingly smooth and muscular, it makes sense of an otherwise enduring mystery, namely the popularity of rye-and-ginger and seven-and-seven, those boring standbys of the curling club and nineteenth hole. Combine two big measures of blended whisky with three dashes of Angostura bitters, over ice, in a chilled collins glass. Fill with ginger ale and garnish with a long twist of lemon peel.

A little breeding can make a big difference. The bitters and lemon lift the familiar mix into a sparkling winner, going away. Get that Neck down yours. It's a cert; a lock; a sure thing.

THE DANDY

The word *dandy* is of eighteenth-century origin, the OED tells us, and may allude to a certain character, Andrew, in a now-forgotten work called *Jack-a-Dandy*. The Oxford lexicographers offer a definition of Andrew and his ilk – "a man unduly devoted to smartness, esp. of clothes" – which seems to us rather prim and judgmental. Dandies, after all, are *unduly* devoted to smartness only from the point of view of schlubs and boors. The fashion-section vogue for metrosexuals and just-gay-enough men has thankfully passed, but leaves in its wake, we hope, real men who not only watch sports but also possess style.

Dandies come in many guises, from sprightly spatted Settembrinis and Astaires to glam gutter-boys like Rilke or Lou Reed, but their core is always intelligence. After all, it's not a coincidence that "smart" means both brains and style. Knowing about, drinking, enjoying, and (sometimes) mixing cocktails are essential skills of the well-rounded man, and you needn't be a total clothes horse to appreciate that the right suit makes your "smart see-through," as one acquaintance likes to call the gibson, that much smarter.

A dandy cocktail should annex your basic brain-wattage, cleaving open a skull tap with the first cold sip, letting the air in and the badinage, flirting, and offhand poetic insights out. Sitting there at the bar, clad in smooth Italian wool, you should be on guard to strike up conversation with any pretty girl who happens to be ordering a sidecar. (Try complimenting her handbag or shoes. Never fails.) Here are some perfect stylish cocktails to make it all happen.

For beginners, the Dandy Cocktail simpliciter. That's three parts Canadian whisky and three parts Dubonnet, a dash Angostura bitters, and three dashes Cointreau; shake well with ice and strain into a chilled cocktail glass. Garnish with a twist each of lemon and orange. Tasty as a good manhattan, and reliable. But if you're a charmer, try a Charmer. Three parts scotch join one part blue curaçao, a dash of dry vermouth, and a dash of orange bitters, all shaken with cracked ice and strained into a chilled cocktail glass. The resulting colour, a sort of dark teal, is an added bonus, *teal* being one of those words, like *lovely*, *sweet*, or *fabulous*, whose casual use marks out the confident dandy. Charmers also fairly wallop, despite the sweet name.

The Fine and Dandy Cocktail is just what it says, being a citrusy mix of four parts gin with two parts each of Triple Sec and fresh lemon juice, plus a dash of orange bitters. (*The Savoy Cocktail Book* subs Cointreau for the Triple Sec and Angostura bitters for the orange, which can be hard to come by.) Shake languorously but thoroughly with cracked ice, then strain into a chilled stem-cone. A very palatable alternative for the habitual martini drinker, with a little more complexity than your usual glass of cold juniper rocket-fuel.

How about a Tuxedo Cocktail for that fabulous night out on the tiles? That's four parts gin, three parts dry vermouth, a half teaspoon of maraschino liqueur, and a dash of orange bitters. Mix, shake, strain. Garnish with a maraschino cherry. This drink, with its big glug of vermouth and fruit sweetness, is actually a variant on the original martini, a drink far sweeter than the bone-dry mixes most people throw back now that gin actually tastes good. If you fancy something completely different, cross over with a nimble Foxtrot: five parts light rum, two dashes of orange curaçao, and the juice of one lime, all mixed with ice and strained into a cocktail glass. A taste from dance palaces of yore.

Speaking of old-school elegance, the most complete dandy we ever came across was a Yale University mannequin who used to sport wasp-waisted seersucker suits, celluloid collars, and spats, even though it was the 1980s and not the 1890s. You can gesture in the same direction, without going as far as spats, by ordering a Cablegram. Just tell the barman to mix four parts blended whisky, one part fresh lemon juice, and a half teaspoon of bar sugar in a chilled collins glass. Add ice and top up with ginger ale. A long cool message from another era.

Or there's always the Knickerbocker Cocktail, another near-cousin of the original martini. Four parts gin are joined by two parts dry vermouth and a half teaspoon of the sweet variety. Stir gently with ice in a mixer, then strain into a chilled cocktail glass. Garnish with a twist of lemon. There's a Knickerbocker Special, too, though it's a very different animal: four parts light rum, a half teaspoon of Triple Sec, and then a teaspoon each of orange juice, lime juice, pineapple syrup, and raspberry syrup. Not worth the trouble, we say.

Stick, instead, to something cool and easy, like the Knockout. Tell the barman to combine four parts each of gin and dry vermouth, plus two parts Pernod and a couple of teaspoons white crème de menthe. Stir with ice and strain into a chilled cocktail glass. "It's a Knockout," you can say to the curious girl eyeing your order. "And may I say? So are you."

TUNNEY, DEMPSEY

Boxing is not a sport, Joyce Carol Oates declared, because it is not about *play*: one plays football or baseball; one does not play boxing. There may be joy in its execution, the happiness derived from an elegant display of violent talent, but it is more Greek drama than game. "If boxing is a sport," she says in the famous essay *On Boxing* (1987), "it is the most tragic of all sports because more than any other human activity it consumes the very excellence it displays."

Consuming excellence is a byword of this book, too, though minus the tragedy and — we hope — risk of facial injury. But while the punch you drink and the punch you throw have different etymologies, they have similar effects:

imbibing one often entails reeling as if from the other. And it was no mere flight of fancy when Kingsley Amis, in the funniest description of a hangover ever committed to paper, numbered among Lucky Jim Dixon's symptoms the feeling that "he'd somehow been on a cross-country run and then expertly beaten up by secret police."

What a pleasure, then, to find that some powerful concoctions of boozy skill take their names from ring greats. The sweet science of bruising, as Pierce Egan called it, meets the dulcet art of mixing in a quartet of drinks that celebrate the one-two combination of smooth and hard. Keep your gloves up.

First, from Amis again, a reminder of a drink not much in evidence lately, even as its namesake has declined in fame. "What would you say to a Gene Tunney cocktail?" a girl's father asks feckless Robin, nervously visiting the parents in *You Can't Do Both* (1994). "I think it might pack more of a punch than I could cope with," Robin replies, heh heh heh.

A limp line about a stiff drink. If you have succumbed to the relentless marketing of relaunched Plymouth gin – no bad thing – this is the perfect venue for that decorous cousin of the sharper London and Bombay varieties. Mix four parts with two parts dry vermouth, then a dash each of fresh orange and fresh lemon juice. Rattle its insides a little with cracked ice, and strain into a chilled cocktail glass. A well-rounded contender, with just enough pop to snap your head back.

Tunney himself was a smooth customer, a boxing stylist who defeated bullish Jack Dempsey to win the world heavyweight championship in 1926. Tunney survived a rematch the next year when he was given an infamous "long count" to recover from a savage knockdown flurry from Dempsey. In fact, Tunney lost just once in his long career, enduring a brutal beating from Harry "The Pittsburgh Windmill" Greb, who beat him so badly he was in bed for a week, having lost two quarts of blood during the fifteen-rounder. Tunney later credited Greb with teaching him how to win the next time.

Dempsey, meanwhile, was no artist, more the model of a new breed of pugilist plotting the transition from "Gentleman" Jim Corbett and relentless but casual Jack Johnson to the likes of Jake LaMotta and Mike Tyson. Born in Manassa, Colorado, Dempsey was the "Manassa Mauler"; Oates says the term "killer instinct" was coined for him, and describes his outlaw ring manner as "swift, pitiless, always direct and percussive." His heavy hands brutalized, among others, then-champ Jess Willard, who suffered a broken jaw, nose, and cheek, plus six lost teeth, before giving up in a 1919 bloodfest.

The Dempsey Cocktail isn't quite so violent, bearing more kinship with Dempsey's genteel post-boxing success as a Manhattan restaurateur. Take four parts London gin and mix with four parts calvados; add two dashes each of grenadine and absinthe, shake hard, strain, and serve. That's the original 1930s Savoy Hotel version; *The New York Bartender's Guide* subs in Pernod for the absinthe, which is fine, but give the absinthe a try now that it's legal again. Careful, though: two of those and you might need to be saved by the bell.

There's a drink called a Knockout, to nobody's surprise, and it's a similar sort of mix, minus the heavy apple of calvados. Combine three parts gin with three parts dry vermouth and two of absinthe. Add a teaspoon of white crème de menthe, shake with ice, and strain into a chilled cocktail glass. The New Yorkers once again suggest Pernod for the absinthe, plus a shade more gin and a cherry garnish; but why mess with a good thing, especially if it'll kick your ass if you do?

There is no Muhammad Ali cocktail, which is maybe just as well given the sad Parkinson's degeneration of that once-great boxer – a reminder of excellence tragically consumed if ever there was one. So, instead, if you prefer your pugilists fictional, and therefore free from real harm except to your aesthetic sensibilities, please recall that great champion of film and Philadelphia, bane of Apollo Creed and Dragan What's-his-name, the shambling, the inarticulate, the lovable . . . Rocky Balboa.

The Italian Stallion Cocktail – yes, it's true – combines four parts bourbon with two parts Campari and one of sweet vermouth; add a dash of Angostura bitters, shake with ice, strain, and serve up, with a twist of lemon for garnish. Bourbon and Campari? No more implausible than Sylvester Stallone having a long acting career.

ECONOMICS 101

"Economics" comes from *oikos*, the Greek word for dwelling, which is why the phrase "home economics" belongs in the Department of Redundancy Department. But there is an insight buried underneath the confusion, because every aspect of what Carlyle labelled "the dismal science" sooner or later has some impact on your personal gross domestic product. Macro always governs micro, even if household management is, for you, a matter of wine in a bottle versus wine in a box.

How about diversifying your economy with some money-inflected drinks? The secret of all cocktails is that inexpensive ingredients can be made to stretch without breaking the bank.

This book is not in the business of recommending cheap gin, but if it's all your budget committee can requisition, feel confident that a well-composed mix will cover a multitude of fiscal sins. Not for you sudden currency devaluations (a.k.a. Empty Wallet Syndrome) or embarrassing bailouts by the Fed (i.e., your dad). No! With cocktails, the local fun-market is bullish! You are posting quarterly profits with every sip! Here are the rules to drink by:

1. Start with lots of Greenbacks. That's four parts gin, two parts green crème de menthe, and two parts fresh lemon juice, all shaken over cracked ice and strained into an old-fashioned glass with a few ice cubes. You don't need a mint to turn out as many of these as you like; and speaking of which, don't worry, the fresh lemon will cut the cloy of crème de menthe, leaving just depth and a snazzy greenish hue.

2. All returns are subject to tax. Well, unless they're capital gains, corporate profit splits, or massive transfers of wealth from the super-rich to their children. But never mind, thoughts of social injustice will slip from view after an Income Tax Cocktail. Combine four parts gin and three parts fresh orange juice with a tablespoon each of dry and sweet vermouth, plus three dashes of Angostura bitters. Shake with cracked ice and strain into a chilled cocktail glass. Drinking that fast will net you a 40 per cent loss in coherence, compounded hourly.

3. Don't overspend. In Alan Hollinghurst's novel *The Line of Beauty* (2004), a group of friends dines in a fashionable London restaurant, Gusto, right after the 1987 market tumble. The resident bartender, Humphrey, late of the Queen Mary, has concocted an apposite tipple called the Black Monday. "Well, it's, what is it?" one of the friends muses. "It's dark rum, and cherry brandy, and sambuca. And loads of lemon juice. It tastes like a *really* old-fashioned laxative." "I can't drink any more," another responds, "but when I hear that, I don't mind."

Precisely. You don't want a cocktail so odd it makes you ill, especially when you already feel sick about falling stock. A more palatable response to the market's ups and downs, the *bellum omnia omnes* where life is nasty, brutish, and short? The Leviathan Cocktail, possibly so-called because it trades fear for security by surrendering all sovereign power. If that makes no sense, keep drinking until it does. Mix four parts scotch with two parts each orange and lemon juice, and add a table-spoon of simple syrup. Shake it all up with cracked ice, strain into a chilled cocktail glass, and take a big appetitive sip.

4. Look out for Number One. Hobbes wasn't the only one to conclude that self-interest makes an economy go. Bernard Mandeville's 1723 doggerel satire *The Fable of the Bees*, wherein a hive of complaining bees manage to cooper-ate through competition, famously argues that "private vices are public benefits" – something both Adam Smith and your

thirst will eventually second. History is silent on whether the Mandeville Cocktail is in fact an homage to said Bernard, but we do know it is four parts dark rum, four parts light, a table-spoon each of Pernod and lemon juice, plus a glug of grena-dine and a big splash of cola. Combine and shake with cracked ice, then strain into an old-fashioned glass with ice cubes. A rum-and-coke variant, in a way, but far more inter-esting. Long live vice.

It's not really related, but if you're feeling funny, switch that up with a Bee's Knees Cocktail. A better drink, it adds four parts gold rum to one each of fresh orange and lime juice, plus a teaspoon of simple syrup and a few dashes of white curaçao. Mix, shake, strain; garnish the glass with orange peel. That makes for a sweet and sweet-looking drink, something to take your mind off the rate of return.

5. Don't neglect Transcendentalism. Yes, that's right. It was Thoreau who set up a celebrated off-the-grid personal economy at Walden Pond, but it was his pal Emerson – also, as it happens, friend and lifelong correspondent of Carlyle – who penned the essay "Self-Reliance," arguing that the best part of humankind was found in non-material pursuits, the economy of the soul, not the dollar. Eponymous or not, the Emerson Cocktail takes four parts gin, two parts sweet ver-mouth, one part fresh lime juice, a teaspoon of maraschino liqueur and gives it all a good shake with ice. Then through the strainer and into a chilled cocktail glass.

And finally: 6. Charity begins at home. "All sensible people are selfish," Emerson wrote, "and nature is tugging at every contract to make the terms of it fair." Maybe, but most of the time it also takes sympathy and goodwill – not to mention law enforcement. The truth is, pure selfishness eventually self-defeats, and every contract is a reminder that we *can't* self-rely. All successful markets are really cooperatives, because my wealth depends on luck and your agreement to recognize it. Think it over – and, wealthy or not, give back 10 per cent.

Bottom line? It'll do your soul good.

THE CELTIC TWILIGHT

Drinking among the Irish is proverbial, but unanalyzed. The general assumption of continuous Guinness and whisky consumption among Emerald Islers hides deeper questions. Questions such as: How about an Irish cocktail? How about, you know, *mixing it up* a bit. Sure, everybody's Irish on St. Patrick's Day, but does everybody have to drink beer? The Irish bars along Fourth Avenue in New York will be packed, the faux pubs here, there, and everywhere flowing with suds and shots, but where is the cocktail to celebrate the dude who drove the snakes into the sea?

Well, pack up your troubles and start with an Everybody's Irish. This is a smart green cocktail consisting of four parts

Irish whisky plus one part each of green Chartreuse and green crème de menthe. Emerald City, Batman, that's bright! Mix with cracked ice, stir energetically, and strain into a chilled cocktail glass. This drink looks better than it tastes, we must say, but not at all bad for those with a sweet tooth.

If whisky's not your cup of tea, switch to gin and fix yourself an Emerald Isle Cocktail. Who says gin is just for the English? Throw five parts of the stuff together with two teaspoons of green crème de menthe and three dashes of Angostura bitters. Stir in your mixing glass with a generous handful of cracked ice, then strain into a chilled cocktail glass. This may be the only cocktail in existence that calls for garnish with a green maraschino cherry, an item otherwise found only on Christmas cakes or cookies. Toss it in anyway – a cheeky touch of blarney.

For those who recall the strong connection between Ireland and the west coast of Scotland, a tribal link responsible for, among other things, the fact that a Glasgow soccer team is called Celtic and sports green shamrocks, commit the nearly unthinkable and mix Irish and Scotch whisky in one glass. The Irish Kilt still favours the former, at four parts to two, so it's a legit St. Paddy's Day mix. Add two parts each of fresh lemon juice and simple syrup, plus three or four dashes of orange bitters, and shake with cracked ice. Strain into a chilled cocktail glass and the result is something between a whisky sour and a sidecar, and delicious all the way down.

Of course, Ireland isn't just the hard-drinking, guff-talking, fist-flying land of lore. It's also the home of a venerable literary tradition that runs the gamut from Wilde to Joyce to Beckett – not to mention Swift, Goldsmith, Berkeley, and Burke. Any country of just a few million that can produce *Lady Windermere's Fan, Finnegans Wake,* and *Waiting for Godot* in a span of just six decades, plus *Gulliver's Travels, She Stoops to Conquer,* and both philosophical idealism and political conservatism, is obviously a place to reckon with.

Behind them all, after his fashion, is William Butler Yeats, poet, dramatist, statesman, and wackjob – the man who founded both the Irish Literary and the Dublin Hermetic societies, won the Nobel Prize for Literature, stirred up political trouble and lost souls alike, and, not least, married an occult-besotted fifteen-year-old called Georgie Hyde-Lees when he was himself a sprightly youth of fifty-two summers. Willie and Georgie together experimented with seances and automatic writing, invoking the spirit world to trace the kooky "gyres of historical change" set out in Yeats's 1925 treatise, *A Vision.*

Yeats was a titan, and if his nuttiness sometimes led him astray, he nevertheless penned some of the greatest lines of the twentieth century. "How can those terrified vague fingers push / The feathered glory from her loosening thighs? / And how can body, laid in that white rush, / But feel the strange heart beating where it lies?" How, indeed?

There is a cocktail called the Celtic Twilight, after the loose brotherhood of Irish writers to which Yeats belonged; but it is a sweet, sticky thing, an ounce each of Irish whisky, Bailey's Irish Cream, and Frangelico, all stirred with cracked ice and then strained over ice in an old-fashioned glass. Blech – a liquid candy bar on the rocks. Brighter by far is the Golden Dawn, named for the famous Order of spiritual adepts W.B. joined later in life. It combines four parts gin and four parts orange juice with two parts each of fresh lime juice and apricot liqueur. Add a dash of grenadine, shake with cracked ice, and strain into a chilled cocktail glass. Excellent for brunch if not for dawn, and guaranteed to make the spirits speak.

In high school a certain English teacher, a Jesuit priest, once unwisely let slip to a roomful of adolescent boys a telling biographical detail. Yeats, he told us, a man who hated death with a passion and had that nubile wife thirty-seven years his junior, raged and lusted well into old age. In the dark pre-Viagra days of the 1930s, "The Circus Animals' Desertion" isn't just about a fading poetic muse. Eventually Yeats resorted to various quack cures and gonadal boosts. To restore the gyres of his transcendental libido, he took to getting regular injections of simian hormone extract. Yes: ape juju juice, one syringe at a time.

We will leave the resulting classroom tumult to the reader's imagination and just note, as a close to this green day, that the

Monkey Gland Cocktail – we are not kidding – combines four parts gin with two parts orange juice, three dashes each of grenadine and absinthe, and, after a good shake over ice, is strained into a chilled cocktail glass. Drink, don't inject. Peace, if not schwing, will come dropping slow.

MARIPOSA

According to Stephen Butler Leacock, who had one in economics, the Ph.D. degree is what they give you when you have demonstrated you are "no longer capable of learning anything."

In this, as in most things, the legendary Canadian humorist was right. He was right that banks are "rattling" places, where even the most sanguine depositor can become "an irresponsible idiot." He was right about the basic fact of public lectures, which we might call Leacock's Law of Diminishing Returned Humiliation: "There are seventeen people present. The lecturer refuses to count them. He refers to them afterwards as 'about a hundred.'"

That axiom surely takes its place alongside anything set down in Leacock's *Elements of Political Science* (1906) or *Practical Political Economy* (1910), two volumes that qualify as his only titles that can be read without pleasure. Not that anyone bothers reading them at all these days. Scholars know that the sage of Orillia was also an economist of considerable gifts, head of the department at McGill University for many years.

People call Leacock a satirist, but he isn't really. Satire, as the humorist Ian Frazier defines it, is writing whose "preferred outcome would be for its object to fall down dead." Leacock rarely wants anyone dead – though he does confess, in the rumination on public lectures, that he "nearly had the pleasure of killing a man with laughing." Rather his comprehensive genius is one of inspiring compassion. There is no darkness in Leacock's universe, though there is plenty of pathos.

His influence is massive. Robertson Davies' rollicking early novels are unimaginable without his example, Salterton (Kingston) being thus a short stop down the district line from Mariposa (Orillia). So are the cult-fare Trailer Park Boys, especially brain-dead Ricky and his pal Julian, a man never without rum-and-Coke in hand, who forever live in the state described by one Leacock character as "idiot hope."

Which brings us, aptly, to drink. Humour is like liquor in ways both obvious and subtle. The good stuff is hard to come by, because difficult to fashion. It intoxicates, but also harrows; it allows truth to flow into places otherwise barricaded.

Sometimes it's champagne, sometimes whisky. And sometimes, as with Leacock, it's a strong fizzy combo.

"There is a sort of convention that when men go fishing they must have whiskey," the narrator of a Leacock tale notes. "Each man makes the pretence that the one thing he needs at six o'clock in the morning is cold raw whiskey. It is spoken of in terms of affection. One man says the first thing you need if you're going fishing is a good 'snort' of whiskey; another says that a good 'snifter' is the very thing and the others agree, that no man can fish properly without a 'horn,' or a 'bracer,' or an 'eye-opener'. . . ."

"The Old, Old Story of How Five Men Went Fishing," source of that wisdom, is "a plain account of a fishing party. Nothing happens in it and nobody is hurt." Indeed, the premise of all Leacock fishing stories is that *nobody ever goes fishing*. The best fish are not caught but snagged, late at night and well away from the water. And here a cool cocktail is your best tackle.

"The number of huge fish that have been heaved up to the top of the water in our lakes is almost incredible," the narrator marvels as he watches a man spread his hands approximately a cubit apart while addressing a group of pals propping up the bar. "Or at least it used to be when we still had bar rooms and little tables for serving that vile stuff Scotch whiskey and such foul things as gin Rickeys and John Collinses. . . . [T]here was good fishing in the bars all winter."

The rickey and the collins have been mentioned here before, but only in passing. A rickey is just four parts gin plus some fresh lime juice and sparkling water, over ice. The John Collins, like its cousin Tom, is lemon juice, simple syrup, and sparkling water plus four parts of your preferred spirit – in this case, blended whisky. Both drinks supply excellent stores of lightness and wallop during the winter fishing season, and the real one.

In honour of a great funnyman and bass-fancier, try something in the same class but even better: the Whisky Sangaree.

Like rickeys, collinses, and slings, a sangaree can be made with various spirits; together with flips, fizzes, and shrubs, it is also among the oldest mixed drinks we know. The name is a corruption of the Spanish sangria, that tasty blood-red mix of wine, fruit, and ice. The original English sangarees featured sherry or port plus ice and spices. This one is rounded out by blended Scotch or Canadian whisky, and that makes it a cocktail. In the bottom of a chilled old-fashioned glass, dissolve half a teaspoon of bar sugar into a teaspoon of water. Add four parts Famous Grouse or C.C., according to taste, and stir. Drop in a few ice cubes, fill with sparkling water, and then float a generous dollop of ruby port on top.

Snort, snifter, horn, or bracer, that'll fix you right up, any time of day.

EAST IS EAST

S hanghai is a city of some 20 million souls, more or less: the vagueness arises because nowadays nobody really knows where the sprawling megalopolis, showcase of juggernaut twenty-first-century China, ends. It just goes and goes, mile after mile of packed high-rise density and sweeping concrete superhighway.

The name Shanghai means "up from the sea," and the city has always offered a powerful point of access to the Sea of Japan and points east. It has likewise proved an irresistible target for Japanese aggression, not least the Second World War sacking that is depicted in J.G. Ballard's *Empire of the Sun* (1984) – in Steven Spielberg's 1987 film version, perhaps

Christian Bale's best non-*Batman* performance, even though he was just a tyke.

Both novel and film show the layered strangeness of Shanghai, its palimpsest of cultural and political claims. During the 1930s, it was a notorious visa-free zone and attracted international gangsters and villains of every description, including the respectable ones known as bankers, who built the grand art deco changing houses that line the Puxi shore of the city, the Bund. The famous Peace Hotel, resting place of exiled emperors, film stars, and rich scoundrels, stands among them still, in all its shabby glory, at 20 Nanjing Lu. Just as Cole Porter is said to have composed "Night and Day" while living in Cleveland's strange old Alcazar Hotel, so Noel Coward allegedly wrote *Private Lives* while on an extended stay at what the Shanghainese call "Ha Ping Fan Dian."

There are cocktail bars aplenty in modern Shanghai, some of them heaven-sent spaceships hovering atop skyscrapers and towering eighty-storey hotels. Here you can observe the burgeoning Chinese plutocracy at play, yelling at waiters and ordering thousand-dollar bottles of champagne. But there is, even better, a dim leather-stitched saloon on the ground floor of the Peace. Here the Old Jazz Band offers a nightly banquet of songbook standards. That "old" covers the band as much as the repertoire. The slinky hostess, a long-limbed babe with a picture-perfect face and dead eyes, hands you a flyer that lists the players' increasingly implausible birthdates. Drummer Mr.

Cheng Yue Qiang was born on June 21, 1918; he rattles the skins pretty efficiently night after night, for an octogenarian. The rest of the sextet is spry by comparison, born during Shanghai's first boom in the 1920s. Pianist Mr. Zhang Jing Yu is the baby of the bunch at just sixty-six.

"Time goes by," the flyer informs you, "memory is forever." Who knows whether the band's short-term memory is even extant, but they certainly grind out the familiar tunes with nary a wrinkle. Outside, Shanghai is a riot of neon and runaway capitalism. In here, it's possible to close your eyes and imagine it is 1928, the dollar and the liquor equally strong, and your enemies momentarily foiled by the clever move of Shanghai-ing yourself to Shanghai.

Time for a manhattan and a cigar, you say. China is, blessedly, one of those places where the evils of tobacco are actually encouraged by the state: just one minor irony of an authoritarian Communist regime in love with Western money and luxury goods. But don't have a plain old manhattan, marvellous though it is as a sip alongside your smoke. You are in the fabled East – or imagining yourself there, anyway – and you deserve something a little more romantic. Ignore for now all those arguments about the cultural construction of the exotic, or the oppressive orientalism of the Westerner abroad. Just remember that there are no more dedicated capitalists alive than the Chinese bankers standing down the bar a step, and order a Shanghai Cocktail.

It is a manhattan relative, really, which means it will still complement your Monte Cristo nicely. Six parts Canadian whisky join two parts sweet vermouth, two parts fresh lime juice, and one part Cointreau in the (if you have one) art deco cocktail shaker. Add cracked ice, shake along in time with the band's rendition of "Smoke Gets in Your Eyes," and strain into a chilled cocktail glass. A twist of lime to garnish is optional. This smart, neglected drink has all the richness of the manhattan but with those sharp added citrus notes of lime and orange. If you find it too sweet, use dry vermouth instead of sweet; or, as with a Perfect Manhattan, go with one part of each.

Perhaps because there are many Shanghais, there are many Shanghai cocktails. Our version is from *The ABC of Cocktails*. *The Savoy Cocktail Book* offers a completely different drink: four parts Jamaica rum, three parts lemon juice, one part anisette, plus two dashes of grenadine; shake and strain into a cocktail glass. (*The New York Bartender's Guide* is similar, just using Pernod instead of anisette – as far as we know, no difference at all.) But these rum-and-lemon combos are too bright for nighttime intrigues. If you want a pick-me-up rather than a pull-me-down, why not shift locations entirely while nevertheless staying in the Exotic East. You can't spit on the sidewalks in repressive Singapore these days – unlike Shanghai, where it is almost an official sport – but you can still order a Singapore Sling, that old favourite of dive bars everywhere.

The true article is actually pretty good, if a little fussy: six parts gin, two parts cherry brandy, two parts fresh lemon, and a teaspoon of bar sugar. Mix everything but the brandy together with ice, strain into a chilled collins glass, and fill with sparkling water and ice cubes. Float the brandy on top, and garnish with an orange-cherry flag.

Never the twain shall meet? These two superb East–West drinks beg to differ.

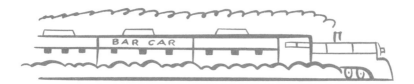

THIRD RAIL

A certain editor from the *New York Times*, who shall go nameless (she knows who she is), has a tattoo on her shoulder in the form of a New York City subway token, the distinctive brassy disk that is for many people the surest image of Manhattan dwelling: all that time spent underground, trying to get from one place to another.

Not even a devoted New Yorker would call it salubrious down there. There are rats, muggers, garbage, and – if recent Hollywood movies are anything to judge by – all manner of superheroes and archnemeses doing fearsome battle. There might even be, as in London or Madrid, the real terror of bombs. Nevertheless, a subway is to a city what veins and arteries are to you and me, and the big metropolis could no more survive without its subterranean maze of rail and tunnel than a body could function absent its lavings of tube-carried blood. William Harvey's early-modern discovery of circulation of the blood offered not just a biological insight, but a general metaphor for urban life. As we all know, in the land of constant movement, gridlock is equivalent to death.

Far be it from this book to suggest how best to pursue your own projects of circulation and body-maintenance, but in the interests of health, a few fast-moving drinks, including one actually non-alcoholic one, will succeed in getting the juices flowing. After all, one purpose of the smart cocktail, as with the classical aperitif, is to slide down the gullet with a bit of a jolt. This lets the physical frame know that food is on its way. A cocktail is your signal train. Just don't let your car get hijacked by bandits, as in the runaway 1974 Robert Shaw heist film *The Taking of Pelham 123* – otherwise known as drinks for dinner.

To snap the bodily system awake, consider the life force of the subway system: the *third rail*. It's the one you don't want to step on, the one that carries the current. The Third Rail Cocktail has a similar voltage – so much so, in fact, that it's not for everybody. Four parts brandy join four parts apple brandy in your shaker with cracked ice. Add one part light rum and a little slug of Pernod, say a quarter teaspoon. Shake well and strain into a chilled cocktail glass. Note that there is a heavy-duty brandy-and-brandy hangover coming down the line with this drink if you don't mind the gap between thirst and sense.

Not many non-alcoholic cocktails find our favour, as a general thing, but mindful of health and still below street level, try a Subway Cooler for a tall summer tipple that won't derail you. That's four parts cherry cider mixed with eight parts fresh orange juice, poured over ice cubes and topped up with ginger ale and a maraschino cherry for garnish. A cousin to Shirley Temple, obviously, and just as you can liquor up the latter with some vodka, creating the Shirley Temple Black, feel free to do the same with this tall drink. Call the result the A Train, which runs all the way from Harlem to the beach at Far Rockaway.

Trains and cocktails seem to go together like the Baltimore and Ohio, so you might want to leave the city above-ground, instead of under it, on an American Flyer out of Grand Central or Penn Station. The namesake cocktail has three parts light rum, a tablespoon of fresh lime juice, and half a teaspoon of simple syrup, all shaken with cracked ice, then strained into a chilled white-wine glass. Top it off with champagne or good sparkling wine. Fresh and bright. You can tone down this Flyer a bit – into, let's dub it, a PF Flyer, after the kids' classic running shoe – by keeping the bubbly but replacing the rum with cider. Or you can go to a different platform altogether and catch a Silver Streak. The films of this name couldn't be more different. The 1934 version is a gripping Chicago-to-Boulder-Dam thrillride involving a fast train, a boy suffering from infantile paralysis, and the iron lung that will save him. Nineteen-seventy-six's *Silver Streak* is an almost-forgotten Gene Wilder/Richard Pryor semi-comedy about murder on a Los Angeles–New York ride, a film meant to pay homage to everything from *North by Northwest* to Bob Hope's goofy comedies but which ends up, according to the *New Yorker*, "a fake thirties mystery comedy . . . so inept you can't even get angry."

Not so the drink, which is just six parts gin and three parts Jägermeister shaken with ice and strained into a chilled cocktail glass. Subbing one part fresh lemon juice for one of the Jägermeister parts makes a Silver Bullet, not to be confused with the beer of the same nickname. As a rule, we do not favour newfangled – or anyway newly fashionable – ingredients such as Jägermeister, too often the preferred tipple of bar-hopping frat boys, who figure they can mix it with everything from beer to Red Bull, but this Silver Streak is a new train worth taking. The gin does it, taking the edge off the stag-hunter's brew and leaving the herbal and aromatic character.

Flyers take to the air as well as the rails. So while we're soaring along, how about airlifting an old favourite from the early days of hotel-bar drinking? The Aviation Cocktail is alive and aloft in *The Savoy Cocktail Book*, whose simple recipe calls for two-thirds dry gin to one-third fresh lemon juice, plus a couple dashes of maraschino liqueur. A slightly more elaborate but better version is four parts gin to one part fresh lemon and a half teaspoon each of maraschino and apricot brandy. Shake and strain into a chilled cocktail glass, and you have a bracer for the start of any sortie over enemy lines.

As always, remember to fasten your seat belt and return your seat and tray-table to their upright position. No matter how carefully you steer, there's always some risk of clear-air turbulence. In which case, you may want to compensate with (or just take solace from) a Tailspin Cocktail. Not for first-time soloists, this dizzy drink calls for four parts gin, three parts sweet vermouth, and three parts green Chartreuse. Splash a dash of orange bitters and you're ready to barrel-roll the works around in your shaker with some ice, then strain into a chilled nose-cone. Garnish with a lemon twist.

Knocked for a loop? Maybe more like an Immelmann Turn, the one where you pull upside-down and end up flying back the way you came. Subway to sublime!

THE GREEN ROOM

G reen rooms are rarely green any more, if they ever were, but the conventional name sticks, as it does in white sale (of things only some of which are white) and blue pencil (which means to edit even though often no actual pencil, blue or otherwise, is nowadays involved). Actors and performers know that the green room is any little place where they stick the talent after makeup and before calling them onstage, onto the set, or into the studio. Nice green rooms have snacks and drinks; nasty ones have burnt coffee and old magazines. It probably goes without saying that, considered globally, most green rooms are not nice.

The writer Christopher Hitchens, a green-room veteran, uses them to make long-distance phone calls and, when possible, take the edge off his hangover with some free libation, for preference white wine. According to the Hitchens Principle, or HitchPrin, no amount of white wine consumed at any time of day constitutes actual *drinking*, which heinous act must involve hard liquor. Hitchens, a litre of white wine at his hand, to a young colleague about to consume a martini after a television interview: "Ah, you remind me of my youth, when I could *drink*." It follows that cocktails are a form of *drinking*, and should be approached with suitable caution and only after careful consideration.

The Green Room Cocktail is not green either, and so must derive its name not from hue but from some association with the noble thespian art – possibly to do with actors' well-known penchant for brandy. Two parts of the distilled grapey stuff, any old kind will do, join four parts dry vermouth and a few dashes of Triple Sec in your shaker, with the usual handful of cracked ice. Stir decorously, then strain into a chilled cocktail glass; garnish with a twist of orange peel. A smart little drink, nicely balanced if rather on the dry side, a sort of metropolitan for grown-ups, and the perfect pick-me-up for those about to tread the boards. Just one, mind you. After all, you are *drinking*.

Playhouse associations mark out a nice line in things to *drink*, in fact, in the green room or after the show. Take the

Matinee Cocktail, a sophisticated mix of four parts gin, two parts sweet vermouth, and a part each of green Chartreuse and fresh orange juice. Add a dash of orange bitters and shake with cracked ice. Strain into a chilled cocktail glass and you have a show that will brighten up any afternoon. Or flash the Broadway Smile, an old-fashioned layered drink of the sort these days mostly found as shooters in the kind of bars we don't go to. The *Savoy Cocktail Book* notes that two parts each of crème de cassis, Swedish Punsch, and Cointreau are carefully poured into a liqueur glass so that ingredients do not mix. Best to drink that in one go, and yes, it will put a grin on your face, even if your pearly whites are not destined to make it onto Broadway.

Mary Pickford was, and later in many a film too. Canadians like to remind the world that before she charmed us as *Rebecca of Sunnybrook Farm* (1917) and *Coquette* (1929 – her first talkie), and so became "The World's Sweetheart," Pickford was just plain Gladys Mary Smith of Toronto, arriving there to her delighted parents in 1893. It's a long way, not only in miles, from Yonge and Bloor to the founding of United Artists and life at Pickfair with Douglas Fairbanks, Sr., but we like to think gorgeous Mary never forgot the Big Smoke north of the border. Her eponymous cocktail has no obvious Canadian or Hollywood resonances, but it's a tasty wee number nonetheless. Four parts light rum are mixed with four parts pineapple juice and a half teaspoon each of grenadine and maraschino liqueur. Shake, strain, and serve in a chilled cocktail glass. Fresh, bright, and sassy.

Enrico Caruso is probably, even in this age of the Three Tenors, the most famous opera singer who has ever lived, his name synonymous with vocal greatness. He could also act, which no Pavarotti, Domingo, or Carreras can claim, and is why his name gets a place of honour here. Sure, Dame Nellie Melba – whose stage name, trivia buffs, was derived from her hometown of Melbourne, Down Under, where she was born ordinary Helen Mitchell in 1861 – has that famous peach and ice cream dish named after her; but our man Enrico, pride and joy of Naples, has the Caruso Cocktail. A sort of martini cousin, it calls for four parts gin, one part dry vermouth, and – here's the continental twist – one part green crème de menthe. Stir in a mixing glass with cracked ice and strain into a chilled cocktail glass. Sing? You'll be hitting high notes all night long.

They call Broadway the Great White Way and we can't laud the world of stage and screen without a proper tribute thereto. There are various drinks named for New York streets – the Park Avenue and the Fifth Avenue cocktails come quickly to mind – but strangely enough there is no Broadway Cocktail. Enter, stage right, the White Way Cocktail, a snappy combination of four parts gin and two parts white crème de menthe. Shake, strain, serve. Simplicity itself, basically a stinger made with gin instead of brandy. The related vodka substitution is just called a vodka stinger, but you could think of it instead as the

Moscow Theatre stinger, a name that combines dramatic art and, in the shadow of the 2002 Chechen siege of the famous playhouse, a hint of explosive danger – Stinger being, among other things, the name of an air-to-air missile. If you like stingers, give these gin or vodka variants an audition and see if it doesn't project right to the back of the house.

Next, a crooked tribute to a woman who wrote for the screen as well as books and for magazines. Dorothy Parker knew a lot about drink, and about getting drunk, and is remembered, among other things, for that much-quoted line about finding oneself, after three drinks, under the table, and, after four, under the host (fair cop if you've been paying attention: yes, that is the second time this book has used the line). Parker wrote poetry, essays, plays, and screenplays. She never acted, at least not on stage or screen, but her film credits included work on the screenplays for Lillian Hellman's *The Little Foxes* (1941), a classic Bette Davis vehicle. Even more extensively, she was a main writer for the original, non-musical version of *A Star Is Born* (1937), that searing portrait, in early colour, of the very Hollywood which was busy making Mary Pickford a star. The 1954 Judy Garland/James Mason remake of the film, still less the gruesome 1976 Barbra Streisand/Kris Kristofferson/Gary Busey disaster ("A bore is starred," said the *Village Voice*), both lack the punch of the original, which has a nifty self-loathing glee to it. The *New Yorker*, a magazine that Parker helped to shape in its early years, would describe this film as "a peculiar sort of masochistic self-congratulatory Hollywood orgy," some parts of which indictment surely apply equally well to poor old Dorothy herself.

Dorothy Parker died alone in a Manhattan apartment – alone, that is, except for her standard poodle, Troy, who stood faithfully by her side. The sad demise of a great woman came after six sustained decades of drink, debt, marriages, affairs, abortions, suicide attempts, and arguments with Robert Benchley, her great love. Benchley, the drama critic, writer, and cameo actor, was a hero to E.B. White, James Thurber, and a host of lesser writers. Parker called him "a kind of saint." He was no stranger to overindulgence himself, getting himself fired from both *Life* magazine and the *New Yorker* for too much imbibing between, sometimes during, theatre reviews. He and Parker were locked, for most of their lives, in blistering rounds of that fatal hopeless violent love we nowadays call co-dependency.

But that was later. In the 1920s, Parker was the toast of the town. Her sparkling put-downs and back-handed compliments defined American wit, especially in the form of deft female evisceration, for a generation or more. Pretty much anything was considered *drinking* in the Algonquin Round Table circles, where all these talented hacks and miniature geniuses habitually foregathered, but here are two drinks to raise in honour of our Dorothy, late and lamented.

First, the Algonquin Cocktail. That's three parts blended

whisky, one part dry vermouth, and one part pineapple juice, all shaken with ice and strained into a chilled cocktail glass. A perfect drink for those who do not want to appear to be drinking, because the pineapple juice, like the O.J. in a screwdriver or Harvey Wallbanger, provides the illusion of health, another sort of willed suspension of disbelief.

Second, consider a drink that might just tie all these loose green-room threads together. Between 1917 and 1920, before she wrote for the *New Yorker*, before the *New Yorker* existed, Parker was theatre critic for *Vanity Fair* magazine, a journal that of course takes its name from the very 1847 novel, written by that regular *Punch* contributor William Makepeace Thackeray, which Parker, having read it at the ripe old age of eleven, later credited for her decision to chase the literary life. *Mirabile dictu!*

"Vanity Fair" is Thackeray's name for the social comedy, which is just the kind of *exeunt omnes* piece that includes things like death from drink. The cocktail is deceptively sweet, like some parts of life's comic arc. Combine four parts apple brandy with two parts kirschwasser, and one part maraschino liqueur, all shaken with ice and strained into yet another handy chilled cocktail glass. Then float a tablespoon of amaretto on top. That's a fruit-and-nut fiesta: apple, cherry, and almonds, all swirling together in one happy hammer of a drink.

We all know that opening night is, sometimes, closing night. But before the curtain goes up, raise your glass like Dot Parker, and dream!

SPYGAMES

Charlie Mortdecai, like the author who created him (Kyril Bonfiglioli), is a former army officer turned shady art dealer who is "loved and respected by all who know him slightly." He is abstemious in all things except food, drink, women, and talking. Also, violent hand-to-hand combat, intrigue, revenge, and theft. Imagine a mix of Oscar Wilde, Bertie Wooster, James Bond, and Quentin Tarantino and you might achieve a fair approximation of this minor literary creation with a major cult following. As with Wodehouse's Wooster, some large measure of the appeal is owing to a memorable, and indispensable, sidekick. In Mortdecai's case, it is his thug, Jock. Any bent art dealer, we learn early on, needs a thug. "Jock is a sort of anti-Jeeves: silent, resourceful, respectful even, when the mood takes him, but sort of drunk all the time, really, and fond of smashing people's faces in."

Mortdecai is not a spy per se, but close enough given the international travel, gunplay, and worldwide conspiracies that figure in the three novels Bonfiglioli left the world before calling last orders in 1985. (There was a posthumous attempt by Craig Brown to offer one further Mortdecai novel, a not-so-noble failure.) You can pick up a fair bit of lore in these books – if not the professional tradecraft of John le Carré, then lots of juicy tidbits about art fraud, sidearms, cookery, and drink. As cocktail enthusiasts go, in the shadowy world of the semi-legal at least, Mortdecai puts George Smiley's gin-and-tonic, even Bond's shaken-not-stirred vodkatinis, in the shade.

"As a serious gastronome I deplore cocktails of course," Mortdecai avers at one point in *Don't Point That Thing at Me* (1973), "but then I also deplore dishonesty, promiscuity, inebriety and many another good." That's why he has five – count them – White Ladies before lunch in Jules's bar off Jermyn Street. Mortdecai is mainly a scotch whisky man, he tells us, but other mixes make their way here and there into Bonfiglioli's pages, including a breakfast concoction of gin with both sorts of vermouth and some fizzy lemonade ("A quick actor, that drink, gets you to where you live in no time"); and something called a General Montgomery, favourite of

Mortdecai's gorgeous millionaire wife ("a fearful sort of dry Martini and so called because the proportion of gin to vermouth is twelve to one" – presumably a reference to some circa-1944 North African mismatch). There is also one not-to-be-repeated episode on the island of Jersey involving a massive intake of pastis in the company of a defrocked priest, about which the less said the better (but see the introduction to the present book).

Let's take the White Lady for simplicity, whether called up in Jules's bar or mixed by the resourceful Jock. It is a neglected drink – not even included in *The New York Bartender's Guide*, if you can credit that. The Savoyards are spot-on, as usual. Take four parts dry gin, two parts Cointreau, and two parts fresh lemon juice; shake vigorously with cracked ice, then strain into a chilled cocktail glass. The name sounds girly but that is a serious smash to the face, especially before lunch, five or fewer.

If the name is not manly enough for you, how about a Moonraker, taking a cue from the quintessential implausible James Bond film (1979), one of the dire Roger Moore efforts, which *Sight and Sound* magazine described this way: "Conspicuously expensive production values but an unmistakably cut-price plot." There's nothing cut-price about the drink, which predates the film by decades and is a mix of brandy, peach brandy, Quinquina, and absinthe. The Savoy experts stipulate a six-person serving, but scale it down to two parts each of the first three, a dash of absinthe, and some shaking, not stirring, before straining into a chilled cocktail glass.

Speaking of which action, the tiresome Bond line forbidding stirring is disputed by many barkeeps, especially when it comes to gin (shaking, they say, bruises the gin). That issue aside, even the so-called Bond Martini is a controversial property. The films often make it a medium-dry vodkatini: see, for example, Timothy Dalton's painful delivery of this order to comely Carey Lowell in *Licence to Kill* (1979). The actual Bond Martini, as described by author Ian Fleming, is another agent altogether: six parts gin, two parts vodka, one part Lillet blanc, all shaken vigorously and strained into a chilled cocktail glass with a twist of lemon for garnish. The Lillet adds nice complexity to all that white spirit, but you might want to go further – change sides, in fact – and mix a KGB or Kremlin Cocktail instead.

The first is two parts kirschwasser, four parts gin, and half a teaspoon of brandy, all shaken and strained into a chilled cocktail glass. Garnish with a lemon twist. The second is, suitably, on the vodka side, with four parts of that joined by three parts each of crème de cacao and cream. All that gets blended together with cracked ice, creating a lush sort of vodka smoothie for the Sovietologists in the crowd.

Not so different, and maybe a lot more glamorous, is the Ninotchka Cocktail: four parts vodka, two of white crème de cacao, and one of fresh lemon juice. Shake with ice and strain into a chilled cocktail glass. Just the tipple for a late-night viewing of the 1939 Ernst Lubitsch film of the same name, starring Greta Garbo as the sultry Communist emissary and Melvyn Douglas as the Paris playboy who falls for her. "There is an old Russian saying," Garbo purrs to him at one point, "that the cat who has cream on his whiskers had better find good excuses." Lick your lips, and sip again.

While we're at all this spygaming, we can't resist the adventitious Watergate echo of the Woodward Cocktail. Four parts scotch, one part dry vermouth, and one part grapefruit juice, all shaken and strained into the usual frosty cocktail glass: tastes better than it sounds. Word has it that the actual Woodward would have dispensed with both the vermouth and the grapefruit juice, but you needn't be so basic. Or how about a Pink Panther, a somewhat fussy but worth-it combination of four parts vodka, two parts dry vermouth, two parts orange juice, a slug of cassis, and half an egg white. Shake that up with cracked ice and strain the frothy pastel result into a chilled cocktail glass.

But we can't leave the underworld of crime, intrigue, and intel without a return to something more robust. Dashiell Hammett wrote just one *Thin Man* novel, a 1933 romp that introduced former sleuth Nick Charles and his sassy, sexy wife, Nora, to a grateful world. William Powell and Myrna

Loy milked the characters for six films of mostly descending merit, though never slacking in their affectionate, boozy, wisecracking marriage. In the 1934 original, Nora orders three martinis in a row – that is to say, ordered all at once and then set down in a row – in order to catch up to tipsy Nicky, already conducting a New York speakeasy orchestra as he agitates a chrome cocktail shaker. "It's all in the rhythm," Nick tells her happily. "A manhattan you shake to foxtrot, a bronx to two-step time. A martini you have to waltz."

Later, back in their hotel, where assorted riff-raff and society people have gathered in a party that never seems to begin or end, Nick distributes drinks from a silver tray. "Highballs and cocktails, that's the long and short of it," he says to nobody in particular. "That's a pun. Punsters ought to be punished." There is murder and punishment to come, of course; or rather, several murders, and lots of associated gun- and fistplay. In Hammett's world, drink and detection go together like gin and dry vermouth.

Hammett was an alcoholic himself, and probably died from complications therefrom. His relationship with Lillian Hellman, said to be the model for Nick and Nora, was not without its tragic elements. He was never, any more than Raymond Chandler was, the tough guy he liked to write about. It's cut-rate psychology to say that these characters express a certain inner conflict that booze otherwise palliated, but it is certainly true that all of Hammett's hard-boiled heroes had a fondness of drink in pursuit of crime or its solution — though not many have as much fun as Nick, a man for whom a breakfast drink is known as "a little something to cut the phlegm." Ed Beaumont in *The Glass Key* (1931) favours scotch but orders a manhattan when he's feeling swanky. Sam Spade, in *The Maltese Falcon* (1930), commits the forgivable tough-guy sin of drinking a pre-mixed manhattan from a paper cup in his office after a hard day.

Neither scene surveys into the famous, and otherwise almost word-for-word, film adaptations that came later, wherein Alan Ladd plays Ed in *The Glass Key* (1942) and of course Bogart plays Spade in John Huston's *Maltese Falcon* (1941). (For aficionados, there's also a 1935 version of *The Glass Key*, starring George Raft, and a 1931 version of *The Maltese Falcon*, starring Ricardo Cortez.) But then, the scene where Nick marks time with the cocktail shaker is not in the original novel. Mixing happens in the culture as well as in the shaker.

In a final tribute, then, to an American original who appreciated a cocktail — if ultimately rather too many of them for his own good, a worthwhile note of caution here at the end — let's stipulate a name change. There is no Spade, Hammett, or Thin Man cocktail that we know of. There is, however, an excellent drink that combines gin and scotch, the two favourite quaffs of the Hammett hard-men. We mean the so-called Smoky Martini. That's six parts gin, one part dry vermouth, and a teaspoon of scotch, shaken with cracked ice and strained into a chilled cocktail glass, lemon twist to garnish. (You can also dilute the scotch by washing it around the glass and discarding, rather than mixing in: the Scotch Wash.)

It may never catch on with the rest of the world, but this drink will always be, for us, better known as the Dash Hammett.

"Don't go yet.
Don't go yet. We'll finish the cocktails."
                    – T.S. Eliot, *The Cocktail Party*

GLOSSARY

Absinthe: A highly alcoholic, anise-flavoured spirit made from herbs, including wormwood.

Alexander: Two parts gin, two parts crème de cacao, and two parts light cream all shaken together with cracked ice and strained into a cocktail glass. Served with a sprinkle of nutmeg on top.

Alexander's Sister: A variation on the Alexander that has an extra half ounce of gin and, instead of crème de cacao, either white or green crème de menthe.

Algonquin Cocktail: Three parts blended whisky, one part dry vermouth, and one part pineapple juice. Shake it all with ice and strain into a chilled cocktail glass.

Amaretto: An almond-flavoured liqueur.

American Flyer: Combine three parts light rum, a tablespoon of lime juice, and half a teaspoon of simple syrup. Shake with cracked ice, then strain into a chilled white-wine glass. Top it up with champagne or a good sparkling wine.

Amer Picon: A bitter, orange-flavoured cordial.

Angler's Cocktail: Take four parts gin, add three dashes of Angostura bitters, three dashes of orange bitters, and three dashes grenadine. Shake briefly with cracked ice, then strain into an old-fashioned glass over ice cubes.

Angler's Tonic: The basic Angler's Cocktail served on the rocks, topped with tonic water.

Angostura bitters: Made from a blend of herbs, plant extracts, and spices, it was originally intended to treat stomach conditions, but is now used in many drinks and cocktails.

Anisette: A sweet, low-alcohol, anise-flavoured drink.

Aqueduct Cocktail: Shake together over ice four parts vodka, a splash each of apricot brandy, white curaçao, lemon juice, and lime juice. Strain into a chilled cocktail glass and garnish with a lemon twist.

Aviation Cocktail: Combine four parts gin to one part lemon juice, add half a teaspoon each of maraschino liqueur and apricot brandy. Shake and strain into a chilled cocktail glass.

Baileys Irish Cream: A liqueur made with an Irish whisky and cream base.

Banff Cocktail: Four parts whisky, one part Grand Marnier, one part kirschwasser, and a dash of Angostura bitters. Shake over cracked ice, strain and serve in a chilled cocktail glass.

Bee's Knees Cocktail: Four parts gold rum to one each of orange juice and lime juice, plus a teaspoon of simple syrup, and a few dashes of white curaçao. Mix, shake, strain, and garnish with an orange peel.

Benedictine: A herbal liqueur with a brandy base.

Black Monday: Dark rum, cherry brandy, and sambuca mixed with loads of lemon juice.

Black Velvet: Slowly pour a quarter pint each of cold champagne and stout or porter.

Bling-Bling Special: A champagne cocktail made with Courvoisier and Cristal.

Bloody Caesar: See Caesar.

Bloody Mary: The typical Bloody Mary is two parts vodka, three parts tomato juice, half a part lemon juice, six dashes of Worcestershire sauce, five drops Tabasco, and ground salt and pepper and horseradish to taste. It can be shaken or stirred based on preference. Pour into a tall glass with ice cubes and garnish with a stalk of celery and a lemon wedge.

Bond Martini: Six parts gin, two parts vodka, and one part Lillet blanc. Shake and strain into a chilled cocktail glass with a twist of lemon for garnish.

Boston Cocktail: Shake together three parts gin, two parts apricot brandy, a teaspoon each of lemon juice and grenadine, and cracked ice. Strain into a cocktail glass and serve.

Boston Cooler: Combine four parts light rum, one part lemon juice, and half a teaspoon of bar sugar. Shake with ice, strain, and pour into a highball glass over ice and top up with sparkling water. Stir and garnish with a lemon twist.

Boston Sidecar: One part each brandy, Triple Sec, and lemon juice and three parts light rum. Shake with cracked ice, strain, and serve in a chilled cocktail glass.

Boston Sour: Mix four parts Canadian whisky, two parts lemon juice, a teaspoon of bar sugar, and an egg white. Shake vigorously and strain into a chilled sour glass. Garnish with a lemon-and-maraschino flag.

Bourbon: An American form of whisky, made from corn, wheat, or rye, and malted barley.

Brandy: A spirit distilled from wine or fermented fruit juice.

Brandy Alexander: A variation on the Alexander that uses brandy in place of gin.

Broadway Smile: Carefully pour two parts each crème de cassis, Swedish Punsch, and Cointreau so that the ingredients do not mix.

Cablegram: Pour four parts blended whisky, one part lemon juice, and half a teaspoon of bar sugar in a chilled collins glass. Add ice and top up with ginger ale.

Caesar: A Bloody Mary with a bit of clam juice mixed in. Also known as a Bloody Caesar.

Calvados: An apple brandy named after a region in France in which it was produced.

Campari: A medicinal Italian aperitif allegedly concocted in the 1850s by Gaspare Campari. A bitter drink flavoured by a secret blend of herbs and spices.

Canadian: A variation on the manhattan. Two jiggers of whisky, a couple teaspoons of Triple Sec, a dash of Angostura bitters, and half a teaspoon of bar sugar. Shake with cracked ice and strain into a chilled cocktail glass.

Canadian Daisy: Stir together, over ice, two big shots of whisky with a teaspoon of raspberry syrup and lemon juice. Pour into a chilled highball or collins glass and fill up with sparkling water. Float some brandy on the top and garnish with raspberries (or saskatoons for a truly Canadian touch).

Cantini: Gin and vermouth served in an army-surplus canteen.

Caruso Cocktail: Stir four parts gin, one part dry vermouth, and one part green crème de menthe in a mixing glass with cracked ice and strain into a chilled cocktail glass.

Cavalier Cocktail: A variation on the champagne cocktail: replace the brandy with calvados, an apple-tinged brandy from Normandy.

Celtic Twilight: Put together an ounce each of Irish whisky, Baileys Irish Cream, and Frangelico. Stir with cracked ice and strain over ice into an old-fashioned glass.

Champagne: A sparkling (carbonated) wine named after the Champagne region in France.

Champagne Cocktail: Pour an ounce and a half of brandy over a sugar cube soaked in Angostura bitters in a champagne flute. Fill the rest of the glass with a decent champagne, stir gently, and serve.

Charmer: Mix three parts scotch with one part blue curaçao, a dash of dry vermouth, and a dash of orange bitters. Shake together over ice and strain into a chilled cocktail glass.

Chartreuse: A distilled wine liqueur made from 130 herbs. It comes in two different types: green and yellow.

Cider: A drink made from apples; "hard" cider is alcoholic.

Cointreau: A brand of Triple Sec liqueur.

Cooperstown: Shake together four parts gin, one part dry vermouth, and one part sweet vermouth. Serve with a sprig of fresh mint as garnish.

Coqu'tel: A mix of brandy and champagne. The original champagne cocktail.

Corpse Reviver: A variation of the Bloody Mary with extra hot sauce, Worcestershire sauce, and egg yolks.

Corpse Reviver Number One: Four parts apple brandy, two parts regular brandy, and one part sweet vermouth, shaken hard with ice and strained into a chilled cocktail glass.

Corpse Reviver Number Two: Mix two parts each of Cointreau, dry gin, Kina Lillet, and lemon juice with a dash of absinthe or Pernod. Shake with ice and strain into a cocktail glass.

Cosmopolitan: A cocktail made with vodka, Triple Sec, cranberry juice, and lime juice.

Cranky Canuck: A variation on the whisky sour using rye instead of scotch.

Crème de cacao: A sweet liqueur flavoured by the cacao bean and the vanilla bean. Usually a light-coloured syrup, but it also comes in a dark version.

Crème de cassis: A sweet, red liqueur made from blackcurrants.

Crème de menthe: A sweet, mint-flavoured liqueur that comes in clear or green varieties.

Cuba Libre: Rum, coke, and lime juice poured into a collins glass with ice.

Curaçao: An orange-flavoured liqueur similar to Triple Sec. It is clear originally but colouring is often added.

Daiquiri: Rum and fruit juice.

Dandy Cocktail: Three parts Canadian whisky, three parts Dubonnet, a dash of Angostura bitters, and three dashes Cointreau. Shake well with ice and strain into a chilled cocktail glass. Garnish with a twist each of lemon and orange.

Dash Hammett: See Smoky Martini.

Dempsey Cocktail: Mix four parts London gin with four parts calvados, add two dashes each of grenadine and absinthe, shake hard, strain and serve.

Drambuie: A scotch whisky liqueur made from honey, herbs and spices, and whisky.

Dubonnet: A wine-based aperitif, either red, amber, or white.

Emerald Isle Cocktail: Combine five parts of gin with two teaspoons of green crème de menthe and three dashes of Angostura bitters. Stir in your mixing glass with cracked ice, then strain into a chilled cocktail glass. Garnish with a green maraschino cherry.

Emerson Cocktail: Take four parts gin, two parts sweet vermouth, one part lime juice, and a teaspoon of maraschino liqueur, shake with ice and strain into a chilled cocktail glass.

Everybody's Irish: Stir four parts Irish whisky, one part green Chartreuse, one part green crème de menthe, and cracked ice. Strain into a chilled cocktail glass.

Fine and Dandy Cocktail: Combine four parts gin with two parts each of Triple Sec and lemon juice, plus a dash of orange bitters (although you can substitute Cointreau for the Triple Sec and Angostura bitters for the orange bitters if need be). Shake with cracked ice and strain into a chilled stem-cone.

Fog-Cutter: Mix four parts light rum, two parts gin, two parts brandy, three parts fresh lemon, two parts fresh orange juice, and a teaspoon of almond syrup. Shake with ice and pour over ice cubes into a collins glass. Float a dollop of sweet sherry on top.

Frangelico: A hazelnut-flavoured, sweet liqueur.

Galliano: A banana-flavoured Franco-Italian liqueur.

Gene Tunney Cocktail: Combine in a cocktail shaker four parts gin with two parts dry vermouth, then a dash each of orange juice and lemon juice. Shake with cracked ice and strain into a chilled cocktail glass.

Gibson: Gin with a few dashes of vermouth, at most, garnished with sweet cocktail onions.

Gimlet: Two or three parts gin to one part Rose's Lime Cordial. Shake with ice and serve in a cocktail glass.

Gin: A spirit made from white grain and juniper berries.

Gin and tonic: Roughly equal parts gin to tonic water, garnished with a lime wedge.

Gin Rickey: Pour four parts gin and two parts lime juice over ice into a chilled highball glass and fill with sparkling water.

Gin Smash: An alternative to a mint julep where gin is substituted for bourbon.

Glayva: A liqueur made from whisky, herbs, and citrus.

Golden Dawn: Take four parts gin and four parts orange juice with two parts each lime juice and apricot liqueur, add a dash of grenadine, shake with cracked ice, and strain into a chilled cocktail glass.

Grand Marnier: A kind of Triple Sec made with oranges and cognac.

Greenback Cocktail: Four parts gin, two parts green crème de menthe, and two parts lemon juice. Shake over cracked ice and strain into an old-fashioned glass with a few ice cubes.

Green Chartreuse: See Chartreuse.

Green Room Cocktail: Stir two parts brandy, four parts dry vermouth, and a few dashes of Triple Sec together with cracked ice in a shaker. Strain into a chilled cocktail glass garnished with a twist of orange peel.

Grenadine: A non-alcoholic syrup used to flavour drinks. The name is commonly used to refer to any syrup made from fruits.

Greyhound: Vodka and grapefruit juice, over ice in a collins glass. Ting soda may replace the grapefruit juice to make a Caribbean Whippet.

Habitant: A variation of the Quebec, it uses a little less whisky, but adds lemon juice and maple syrup (about a teaspoon each). It can be garnished with an optional orange-and-cherry flag.

Harvard: Four parts brandy, one part sweet vermouth, a big splash of lemon juice, a splash of grenadine, and a dash of Angostura bitters. Shake over cracked ice, strain, and serve.

Harvey Wallbanger: Mix two big measures of vodka with a modest amount of orange juice in a chilled collins glass. Float a pony of Galliano on top.

Horse's Neck: Add three dashes of Angostura bitters to two big measures of blended whisky in a chilled collins glass over ice. Fill with ginger ale and garnish with a long lemon peel twist.

Hudson Bay: Four parts gin, two parts cherry brandy, one part fresh orange juice, a tablespoon of lime, and a glug of 151-proof rum. Shake hard with ice and strain into a cold cocktail glass.

Income Tax Cocktail: Four parts gin and three parts orange juice with a tablespoon each of dry and sweet vermouth, plus three dashes of Angostura bitters. Shake with cracked ice and strain into a chilled cocktail glass.

Irish Kilt: Combine four parts of Irish whisky with two parts of scotch whisky, add two parts each of lemon juice and simple syrup, plus three or four dashes of orange bitters and shake with cracked ice. Strain into a chilled cocktail glass.

Irish Whisky: A grain whisky made in Ireland.

Italian Stallion Cocktail: Mix together four parts bourbon with two parts Campari and one of sweet vermouth, add a dash of Angostura bitters, shake with ice, strain and serve with a twist of lemon for garnish.

Jack Rose: Shake together four parts applejack or calvados, one part lemon juice, a teaspoon of grenadine, and cracked ice. Garnish a chilled cocktail glass with a twist of lemon and serve.

Jägermeister: A German liqueur flavoured with fifty-six secret herbs.

Jersey Club Cocktail: Mix four parts gin with one part lemon juice, half a teaspoon of white crème de cacao, and a dash of Angostura bitters. Shake with cracked ice and strain into a chilled cocktail glass.

Jigger: A measurement equal to one-and-a-half ounces.

John Collins: Lemon juice, simple syrup, and sparkling water added to four parts of blended whisky.

K.G.B.: Two parts kirschwasser, four parts gin, and half a teaspoon of brandy all shaken and strained into a chilled cocktail glass garnished with a lemon twist.

Kina Lillet: A brand of Lillet blanc.

Kir: A cocktail made with crème de cassis and white wine.

Kir Royale: Nine parts of champagne to one part cassis.

Kirschwasser: A clear brandy made from black cherries.

Knickerbocker Cocktail: Stir four parts gin, two parts dry vermouth, and half a teaspoon of sweet vermouth gently with ice in a mixer, then strain into a chilled cocktail glass. Garnish with a twist of lemon.

Knickerbocker Special: Four parts light rum, half a teaspoon of Triple Sec, and a teaspoon each of orange juice, lime juice, pineapple syrup, and raspberry syrup.

Knockout: Mix four parts each gin and dry vermouth, two parts Pernod, and a couple of teaspoons of white crème de menthe. Stir with ice and strain into a chilled cocktail glass. Alternatively, combine three parts gin with three parts dry vermouth and two of absinthe. Add a teaspoon of crème de menthe, shake with ice, and strain into a chilled cocktail glass.

Kremlin Cocktail: Blend together four parts vodka and three parts each crème de cacao and cream with cracked ice.

Leviathan Cocktail: Take four parts scotch, two parts each orange and lemon juice, and add a tablespoon of simple syrup. Shake it all up with cracked ice and strain into a chilled cocktail glass.

Lillet: A French aperitif wine that comes in either red or white varieties.

Mandeville Cocktail: A more interesting version of the rum and coke. Four parts light rum, four parts dark rum, a tablespoon each of Pernod and lemon juice, plus a glug of grenadine, and a big splash of cola. Combine, shake with cracked ice, then strain into an old-fashioned glass with ice cubes.

Manhattan: A classic manhattan is two parts whisky to one part sweet vermouth with a dash of bitters. It is stirred with ice, strained into a cocktail glass, and garnished with a maraschino cherry.

Man O'War: Four parts bourbon, two parts each Triple Sec and lime juice, and one part sweet vermouth. Mix with ice, shake, and strain into a cold cocktail glass.

Maraschino liqueur: A bittersweet liqueur flavoured with cherries.

Martini: The classic martini is two-and-a-half parts gin to half a part dry vermouth shaken or stirred with ice, strained into a cocktail glass, and garnished with either an olive or a lemon twist.

Mary Pickford: Mix together four parts light rum, four parts pineapple juice, and half a teaspoon each of grenadine and maraschino liqueur. Shake, strain, and serve in a chilled cocktail glass.

Matinee Cocktail: Four parts gin, two parts sweet vermouth, and a part each of green Chartreuse and orange juice. Add a dash of orange bitters and shake with cracked ice. Strain into a chilled cocktail glass.

McClelland Cocktail: Take four parts sloe gin, two parts white curaçao, and a dash of absinthe (or three to five dashes of orange bitters), shake with cracked ice and strain into a chilled cocktail glass. Garnish with a cherry or a lemon twist.

Mint julep: Combine mint leaves and a tablespoon of simple syrup in a chilled highball glass. Bruise the mint leaves to release their flavour and fill the glass with shaved ice. Add six parts of bourbon and garnish with a sprig of mint.

Mojito: The common mojito is a combination of rum, soda, lime juice, sugar, and mint served over ice. For a mojito straight up take four parts light rum, two parts lime juice, a teaspoon of bar sugar, five or six bruised mint leaves, and a dash of Angostura bitters. Shake with cracked ice, strain, and serve in a cocktail glass.

Monkey Gland Cocktail: Shake four parts gin, two parts orange juice, three dashes each of grenadine and absinthe with ice and strain into a chilled cocktail glass.

Moonraker: Two parts each brandy, peach brandy, Quinquina, and a dash of absinthe. Shake and strain into a chilled cocktail glass.

Negroni: One third each of gin, Campari, and sweet vermouth shaken over cracked ice and served in a cocktail glass. Garnish with an orange wheel or twist and optional sugar on the rim.

Ninotchka Cocktail: Combine four parts vodka, two of white crème de cacao, and one of lemon juice. Shake with ice and strain into a chilled cocktail glass.

Orange bitters: An alcoholic preparation with a bitter flavour. It is made from unripe orange peels soaked in alcohol.

Papa Doble: A daiquiri according to Ernest Hemingway: eight parts Bacardi White Label rum, juice of two limes and half a grapefruit, and two dashes of maraschino liqueur mixed with ice and served in a chilled collins glass.

Pastis: An anise-flavoured liqueur and aperitif from France.

Pernod: A brand of pastis.

PF Flyer: A variation on the American Flyer that replaces the rum with non-alcoholic cider.

Pink Panther: Take four parts vodka, two parts dry vermouth, two parts orange juice, a slug of cassis, and half an egg white. Shake with cracked ice and strain into a chilled cocktail glass.

Pony: A measurement equal to one ounce.

Poodle-on-a-Cloud: A margarita served with the glass placed in a soup bowl full of dry ice garnished with a plastic poodle ornament.

Port: A fortified wine that is sweeter and possesses a higher alcohol content than most wines.

Preakness: Mix four parts blended whisky, two parts sweet vermouth, and a teaspoon of Benedictine. Shake together over ice and strain into a chilled cocktail glass garnished with a lemon twist.

Princeton: Six parts gin, two parts ruby port, and three to five dashes of Angostura bitters. Shake, strain, and serve in a chilled cocktail glass garnished with a lemon.

Psychedelic Wallflower: Cointreau and tonic water over ice in a collins glass.

Quebec: Shake six parts whisky, two parts Amer Picon, two parts dry vermouth, and one part maraschino liqueur with cracked ice. Strain and serve in a chilled cocktail glass.

Queen Elizabeth: Stir together over ice, six parts gin, one part dry vermouth, two teaspoons of Benedictine. Strain and serve.

Quinquina: The French name for all bitters that have quinine as part of their main ingredients.

Rattlesnake: Four parts blended whisky with one part lemon juice, a teaspoon of simple syrup, a quarter teaspoon of Pernod, and the white of one egg. Shake over cracked ice and pour over ice in a chilled old-fashioned glass.

Rickey: See Gin Rickey.

Rose's Lime Cordial: The brand name of a sweetened lime juice.

Rum: A spirit made from distilled sugarcane products.

Rum Collins: A variation on the Tom Collins that replaces the gin with rum.

Rusty Claymore: A variation on the Rusty Nail that uses Glayva instead of Drambuie.

Rusty Nail: Four parts blended scotch mixed with two parts Drambuie, over ice in a chilled old-fashioned glass.

Rye: A spirit distilled from rye grain.

Rye highball: A drink made from rye whisky and ginger ale.

Sambuca: A liqueur, usually colourless, flavoured with anise and elderberry.

Saratoga Cocktail: Combine six parts brandy with a splash of lemon juice and maraschino liqueur, add pineapple juice to taste.

Scotch: A type of whisky made in Scotland. Especially whisky made from malted barley.

Shanghai Cocktail: Six parts Canadian whisky, two parts sweet vermouth, two parts fresh lime juice, one part Cointreau. Shake with cracked ice and strain into a chilled cocktail glass. A twist of lime garnish is optional.
   Alternatively, a Shanghai Cocktail can also be four parts Jamaican rum, three parts lemon juice, one part anisette, plus two dashes of grenadine. Shake and strain into a cocktail glass. (You can also substitute Pernod for the anisette.)

Sherry: A type of wine fortified with brandy.

Sidecar: Mix six parts brandy with two parts lemon juice and one part Triple Sec. Shake together over ice and strain into a cocktail glass to serve.

Silver Bullet: A variation on the Silver Streak. Six parts gin, two parts Jägermeister, and one part lemon juice shaken with ice and strained into a chilled cocktail glass.

Silver Streak: Six parts gin and three parts Jägermeister shaken with ice and strained into a chilled cocktail glass.

Singapore Sling: Take six parts gin, two parts cherry brandy, two parts lemon juice, and a teaspoon of bar sugar. Mix everything but the brandy together with ice, strain into a chilled collins glass, and fill with sparkling water and ice cubes. Float the brandy on top, garnish with an orange-and-cherry flag and serve.

Sloe Dick Fizz: Four parts sloe gin, two parts gin, three parts lemon juice, and a splash of syrup shaken together with cracked ice. Strain into a chilled highball or collins glass over ice cubes and fill with sparkling water. Garnish with a lemon slice.

Sloe Gin: A sweet cordial distilled from overripe sloe plums.

Sloe Gin Cocktail: Six parts sloe gin shaken over ice with a teaspoon of dry vermouth and a couple dashes of Angostura bitters. Strain into a cocktail glass.

Smoky Martini: Six parts gin, one part dry vermouth, and a teaspoon of scotch, shaken with cracked ice and strained into a chilled cocktail glass. Add a lemon twist for garnish.

Smooth Cast: A variation on the Angler's Cocktail substituting a tablespoon of Cointreau or Triple Sec for the orange bitters.

Stinger: Four parts brandy and two parts white crème de menthe shaken over cracked ice. Pour into a chilled cocktail or old-fashioned glass.

Subway Cooler: Pour four parts cherry cider and eight parts orange juice over ice cubes in a collins glass. Top up with ginger ale and a maraschino cherry for garnish.

Swedish Punsch: A traditional Swedish liqueur made from arrack (a strong Indian liqueur) and sugars.

Tailspin Cocktail: Shake four parts gin, three parts sweet vermouth, three parts green Chartreuse, and a dash of orange bitters with ice. Strain the cocktail into a chilled nose-cone garnished with a lemon twist.

Third Rail: Combine four parts brandy, four parts apple brandy, one part light rum, and about a quarter of a teaspoon of Pernod in a shaker with cracked ice. Shake well and strain into a chilled cocktail glass.

Tom Collins: Shake two jiggers of good gin, the juice of one lemon, and a spoonful of superfine sugar over cracked ice. Strain into a frosted collins glass or any tall glass filled with ice cubes. Fill the rest of the glass with club soda and garnish with a slice of orange or lime and a cherry if desired.

Triple Crown: Four parts vodka, two parts gold rum, one part each strawberry liqueur and lime juice, and a teaspoon of grenadine. Shake with cracked ice, strain into a chilled cocktail glass, and garnish with a twist of orange.

Triple Sec: An orange-flavoured, sweet liqueur.

Trois Rivières: Combine two big measures of whisky with half an ounce of Dubonnet rouge and a tablespoon of Cointreau. Shake with ice, strain, and serve with an orange twist garnish.

Tuxedo Cocktail: Four parts gin, three parts dry vermouth, half a teaspoon of maraschino liqueur, and a dash of orange bitters shaken, strained, and garnished with a maraschino cherry.

Vanity Fair: Combine four parts apple brandy, two parts kirschwasser, and one part maraschino liqueur. Shake with ice and strain into a chilled cocktail glass. Float a tablespoon of amaretto on top.

Vermouth: A type of fortified wine flavoured with herbs and spices, in dry and sweet varieties.

Vermouth cassis: A drink made with dry vermouth, crème de cassis, and carbonated water.

Vodka: A colourless spirit typically made from grains or potatoes.

Vodka Stinger: Four parts vodka and two parts white crème de menthe. Shake, strain, and serve. A stinger made with vodka instead of brandy.

Whisky: A broad category of spirits distilled from grains (including barley, rye, and corn) and aged in oak casks.

Whisky Sangaree: In a chilled old-fashioned glass, dissolve half a teaspoon of bar sugar into a teaspoon of water. Stir in four parts blended scotch or Canadian whisky (Famous Grouse or Canadian Club, for example), add a few ice cubes, fill with sparkling water, and then add a dollop of ruby port to the top.

Whisky Sour: Mix two big jiggers of decent blended scotch with the juice of one lemon, one lime, a couple teaspoons of fine sugar or plain syrup and a dash or two of bitters. Shake with ice, strain, and serve in an old-fashioned glass or sour glass with a lemon twist garnish.

White Angel: Half vodka, half gin. Shake and strain into a cocktail glass.

White burgundy: A white wine made in the Burgundy region of France.

White Lady: Take four parts dry gin, two parts Cointreau, two parts lemon juice. Shake with cracked ice and strain into a chilled cocktail glass.

White Way Cocktail: Shake four parts gin and two parts white crème de menthe together, strain, and serve. A stinger made with gin instead of brandy.

Winter Angel: Shake six parts vodka with two parts calvados over cracked ice, strain, and serve in a chilled cocktail glass with a lime twist garnish.

Woodward Cocktail: Four parts scotch, one part dry vermouth, one part grapefruit juice all shaken and strained into a frosty cocktail glass.

Yale: A variation on the martini. Add to the standard four-to-one gin and dry vermouth martini a splash of maraschino liqueur and three dashes of orange bitters. Shake with cracked ice, pour into a chilled cocktail glass, and garnish with a lemon peel.

Zombie: Three ounces of rum, one ounce each for light, amber, and dark rums added to some type of tropical fruit juice (pineapple, papaya, mango, for example). A glug of apricot brandy or cherry whisky is optional. Shake it all together and pour over ice in a chilled collins or highball glass. Can be garnished with a cherry or powdered sugar on the rim. Before serving, layer a teaspoon of 151-proof rum on the top.

Credits

Quotations from P.G. Wodehouse, copyright © P.G. Wodehouse. Reproduced by permission of the Estate of P.G. Wodehouse c/o Rogers, Coleridge & White Ltd., 20 Powis Mews, London WII IJN.

"You Hit the Spot" from the Paramount Picture *Collegiate*. Words and Music by Mack Gordon and Harry Revel. Copyright © 1935 (Renewed 1962) by Famous Music Corporation. International Copyright Secured. All Rights Reserved.

The Sun Also Rises by Ernest Hemingway, published by Jonathan Cape. Used by permission of The Random House Group Ltd.

Quotation from 'Leda and the Swan' by W. B. Yeats reprinted by permission of A. P. Watt Ltd on behalf of Gráinne Yeats, Executrix of the Estate of Michael Butler Yeats.

Quotation from *The Cocktail Party* by T. S. Eliot from *Collected Poems and Plays* (Faber and Faber Ltd, 2004) by permission of the publisher.

MARK KINGWELL IS A PROFESSOR OF PHILOSOPHY AT THE UNIVERSITY OF TORONTO, A CONTRIBUTING EDITOR OF HARPER'S MAGAZINE, AND THE AUTHOR OF NINE BOOKS OF POLITICAL AND CULTURAL THEORY. HE ALSO PUBLISHES WIDELY ON ART, FILM, ARCHITECTURE, AND DESIGN. "CLASSIC COCKTAILS" IS BASED ON HIS AWARD-WINNING DRINKS COLUMN IN TORO MAGAZINE.

SETH (GREGORY GALLANT) IS A CARTOONIST AND BOOK DESIGNER. HIS BOOKS INCLUDE: IT'S A GOOD LIFE, IF YOU DON'T WEAKEN, CLYDE FANS, AND WIMBLEDON GREEN.